My Prayer Journey
Lessons Learned

Jane Cottrill

WOODSONG
PUBLISHING

Seymour, Indiana

My Prayer Journey: Lessons Learned
Jane Cottrill

Copyright © Pending 2022 All rights reserved.
Woodsong Publishing
5989 Spring Meadow Lane
Seymour, IN 47274
www.woodsongpublishing.com
woodsongpublishing@yahoo.com

Most Scripture quotations are from the King James Version of the Bible.

Some Scripture quotations are from the following versions: NIV; ESV; AMP.

New International Version®, NIV®. Copyright © 1973, 1978, 1984, 2011 by Biblica, Inc.™ Used by permission of Zondervan. All rights reserved worldwide. www.zondervan.com The "NIV" and "New International Version" are trademarks registered in the United States Patent and Trademark Office by Biblica, Inc.®

English Standard Version: ESV® Bible (The Holy Bible, English Standard Version®), copyright © 2001 by Crossway, a publishing ministry of Good News Publishers. Used by permission. All rights reserved.

Amplified Bible (AMP) Copyright © 2015 by The Lockman Foundation, La Habra, CA 90631.

Cover design by Vision Graphics, Seymour, IN
Printed in the United States of America

ISBN 979-8-9855200-0-2

Dedicated to my beloveds

Carter Matthew
Dylan Paul
Morgan Emilee
Adeline Jane
Blair Elizabeth
Maw Maw loves you all a bushel and a peck.

Out of heaven he made thee to hear his voice, that he might instruct thee: and upon earth he shewed thee his great fire; and thou heard his words out of the midst of the fire.

Deuteronomy 4:36

My Prayer Journey: Lessons Learned

Introduction

Do you remember your first encounter with God? I do. I was nine years old sitting on a back pew next to my twin sister in a rural Illinois small town church when He began to tug on my heart. He made the first move as the saints of God were singing, praising, and praying. That first contact revealed to me that I needed God in a big way. I look back on it now and think about being nine, yet feeling the heaviness of sin and knowing I needed help. I ran to an altar of repentance and began my pursuit on my knees. Over the years I have learned that is the best place to find Him, in prayer. Prayers of repentance; cleaning off the filth of the day, praising Him for meeting me yet again, telling Him my heart weights, and listening for His sweet voice. That is where I find Him. That is where I will learn what I need to know for the day.

In my life's journey I have learned many things through experience, grammar and high school, obtaining a Bachelor's Degree in Christian Education at a Christian college, and an Associate Degree in Nursing as a non-traditional student. I have used what I have learned in those venues to be a wife, raise my boys, teach Sunday school classes for many years, be a helpmeet to my pastor husband, and work in the secular world. But as I enter what is surely the last trimester of my life, I realize that all that I ever really needed to know

I learned sitting at His feet in my prayer closet. Those prayer experiences are what has given me the opportunity to have a relationship with the Almighty. That relationship has affected my marriage, how I mothered, what I taught, and what kind of pastor's wife and nurse I would be.

Becoming the young bride of a God-fearing man has been "the" blessing of my life-time, second only to being filled with His Spirit and speaking in other tongues as the Spirit gave the utterance at the age of twelve. Our journey has not always been easy, not by any stretch of the imagination. We have weathered the storms of poverty, sickness, and insecurity, but through all of these things, God has met me in my prayer closet, sometimes with gentle whispers and hugs, other times with hard cold rebukes that sobered me and turned me around.

When we first became pastor of a fledgling congregation, I had no idea what would lie ahead. The five years we spent in a small town in Ohio in our rented, turn-of-the-20th-century, gray asphalt-shingled home, were wilderness years. We faced great obstacles there which drove me out of want and need, sickness and loneliness, fear and rejection, to my knees on the cold and bare wooden floor of our small second-floor bedroom. Desperate prayers for food, healing, bill-paying money, and fellowship would transform me into feeling full, warm, and content after sitting at His

My Prayer Journey: Lessons Learned

feet in those hours of prayer.

My years of parenting whizzed by on a roller coaster of lightning speed. As the mother of two sons who would give their hearts to Jesus, then explore the world and its offerings, and thankfully return to their roots, establishing their own walk with the Lord, I was propelled into the secret place of the most-High, travailing and interceding for their eternal destinations. As difficult as those days were, I learned that God loved them more than I ever could. I understood that He was their Father and if I would allow Him to parent, He would bring them full circle. I was shown in those early morning hours, lying on my face in a carpet wet with tears, that He heard my prayers, felt my pain, and would intercede.

Teaching Sunday school classes since I was twelve has been a constant joy. I remember taking my first class of toddlers into a room smaller than most closets today, the cherub-like faces listening intently as I used the storytelling gift God placed in me. At eighteen I began teaching fifth and sixth graders, as I do yet today. Teaching them the truths of God's Word has made me dig deep into the Word for myself, praying for understanding and revelation. The dawning of what those kids needed to know would come to me as I sought the throne for a baptism of love for each one of them. Still today their many faces float into my mind's eye, and I hope that the seeds I sowed have produced

fruit in their eternal souls.

Becoming a nurse, and wanting to use that part of my life as ministry, pushed me to many early morning prayer meetings—prayers to let my patients and co-workers see Him in my eyes, feel Him in my touch, and hear Him in my voice. These prayers gave me an awareness of those around me that needed an uplifting word, a prayer for courage, or a hug to make it through their day.

To know the Creator in His ultimate power and glory has been my goal. To nurture relationship with my Savior inspires yet another trip to my prayer place. Understanding Him and hearing His voice has been my desire. Experiencing joy unspeakable and housing the glorious Holy Ghost has been my longing. The longer the trek, the more I have come to realize that He is so big, so strong, so complex, so loving, and so extremely, intimately available. Yet the more I know Him the more I don't know. When I see His majesty in the sunrise, feel the goosebumps of His presence that come to me in praise, or hear that still small voice, I am drawn into that place called prayer and it is there that I can learn all that I really need to know.

It is my desire to share some of what I have learned with you. Prayerfully sit back and digest my experiences, then please go find a quiet place daily and learn all that you ever will really need to know you can learn in your own prayer closet.

My Prayer Journey: Lessons Learned

1 I was a sheltered nine-year-old little girl, growing up in a small white clapboard house my dad built with his own hands. My mom never held a secular job. Her life, her calling, was raising her family of four girls, taking care of our home, providing delicious meals, and caring for my dad. Her mother would eventually move in with us after becoming a widow and not having the means or the health to stay on her own. A third, paneled, linoleum-floored bedroom my dad would add on to our little home, would be grandma's room.

I always knew that my grandma loved Jesus. From my early memories of seeing her faithfully attend church, to the years that she would live out her life with us, she was a praying, Bible-reading woman. I have dim memories of hearing her pray in her bedroom with the door closed. I have thumb nail sketch memories of seeing her read the Word, sometimes with it laying open in her lap as her chin rested on her chest, eyes closed.

It was in this sun-drenched safety that I was raised. I never remember feeling vulnerable, hungry, or poor. Our table was always filled with our own farm butchered meat and vegetables from

our enormous garden. I have no memories of fear, unless you count the time a neighbor's cow wondered up on our stoop in the middle of the night. When my dad went to check on the noise, she poked her unexpected brown and white head in the door. Or maybe the time I slipped and fell on the hay mow steps, dangling upside down until the strong arms of my uncle rescued me and set me aright. I still get a little bit shaky-kneed when walking on open stairs today.

    My days were filled with love, farm chores, wonderful playtimes with my sisters, and singing, yes singing. I can close my eyes and sing along with the record player sounds of the Statesmen Quartet, the Johnson Sisters, and the Happy Goodman's. I particularly remember the beautiful tenor voice of Rosie Rozell blending with the beautiful four-part harmonies.

    As I recollect those carefree, childhood years, and then the abrupt feeling of conviction coming upon me at the age of nine, there is such a contrast. I recall it as if it were yesterday, sitting on the back pew of our church with the blue and brown plaid, cotton dress covering my knees. I do not know what the preacher was saying, but I know I felt lost, sad, and fearful of where I would spend eternity. The conviction of the Holy Ghost was weighing heavy on my heart as I pushed past my bashful personality and started for the altar. I traveled down what seemed like a very long aisle

My Prayer Journey: Lessons Learned

lined with intimidating adult faces watching me. Arriving at the altar I knelt and began to pray, unbidden tears streaming down my little cheeks as I asked Jesus for His help. My grandmother's voice soon came into my awareness, and as she guided me through my repentance, it was there that I fell in love with the God of heaven. Prior to that night, I had said my memorized mealtime prayers and my obligatory bedtime devotions, but I had never experienced what I felt that night.

And so, the journey began on that Sunday night in 1963, kneeling on the shiny, varnished, wooden floor, piano side. I learned I needed Jesus and loved the feeling of forgiveness and love that I had never felt before. I learned that kind of love only comes from Him.

Lesson Learned: I need Jesus.

> But I am poor and needy; yet the Lord thinketh upon me: thou art my help and my deliverer; make no tarrying, O my God.
> Psalm 40:17 KJV

Notes

My Prayer Journey: Lessons Learned

2

At the age of ten my dad packed a thirty-foot U-Haul and my uncle's pick-up truck to leave behind our rural existence. The melancholy emotions were prevalent in all of us. Closing the door on an empty house, a place you have called home, is always strangely surreal. But as a child, wherever my mom, dad, and grandma were going was where I wanted to be, so to me we were setting out on the biggest adventure of my life. We left on an early, hazy, September morning. The air was cool, and a misty rain left droplets running down the car windows as I gazed out and said good-bye to our childhood home. That day we made the drive four and a half hours north to Wilmington, Illinois, which would become our new hometown. Dad, now age thirty-five, was tired of the back breaking inconsistent work he had done as a laborer and was grabbing the opportunity afforded him by his childhood friend to work at the Amoco Chemical plant in Joliet. His decision seemed to be purely based on the employment prospect, but looking back over the years I can see God's hand was directing my footsteps even as a child.

Jean, my twin sister, and I, had been baptized

by our pastor not very long after my life changing repentance. We left that church behind that day, a church of nearly two hundred, quite a large congregation for the time and demographic. My parents were good, hard-working people but were not strongly committed Christians. As far as I know my dad had not sought any kind of godly counsel or checked into churches near our new residence.

A few weeks after settling in, my dad took us to a church in Joliet, sixteen miles from Wilmington. We also went a couple times to the Pentecostal church in Kankakee, Illinois, which was twenty or more miles from our home. Both churches were good-sized United Pentecostal Church congregations. Neither really "felt" right, and with my dad's shift work schedule—working most week-ends—our one-car family did not have the means to attend regularly.

The following month, on a bright Saturday morning, there was a knock on the door. My mother opened it to a slightly built, freckle-faced, red-haired man and his young daughter. They were canvassing the neighborhood and inviting people to their church. The ruddy looking man was Brother Jimmy Galbraith. He had moved his family to Wilmington the previous May to start a church, and they lived just around the corner from us. We quickly became a part of that newly organized congregation.

My Prayer Journey: Lessons Learned

Our first services were at the Masonic Temple Lodge on Sundays. I remember being there a few times with less than twenty people in attendance. The strangeness of the surroundings, with little music, felt odd to me. I do not recall any spiritual experiences there. Shortly thereafter, however, the Galbraith's converted their one-car garage into a sanctuary. An upright piano against one wall, a small podium for a pulpit, and wooden folding chairs—rented from the Masonic Lodge—were all they needed to set up a place for us to worship. Inside the confines of those garage walls, and seated around their kitchen table, being taught Sunday school lessons by Sister Galbraith, my sisters and I began to grow spiritually.

Pastor Galbraith, an Apostolic Bible Institute alumnus, was rooted and grounded in the One-God doctrine and his love for the truth of God's Word. He taught and preached under the anointing and unction of the Holy Ghost, and I would often pray at the little bench he had placed in front of the podium as an altar. I wanted—I needed—the Holy Ghost that the Bible taught was evidenced when you spoke in another tongue. I realized my need of this experience to be saved and wrestled with my desire for more of Him and the need of salvation.

The cold, gray, epoxy-covered, cement floor of the garage would be my second "prayer closet." I would visit there at the close of nearly every Sunday night service. I learned in those meetings

that I would have to continue to die out to the sins of late childhood, and that giving myself entirely to Him was not something I could do on my own. I would need Him for the rest of my life to take control of me but could not yet fully understand how that would happen.

Lesson Learned: I need Holy Ghost power.

> God that made the world and all things therein, seeing that he is Lord of heaven and earth, dwelleth not in temples made with hands; Neither is worshipped with men's hands, as though he needed anything, seeing he giveth to all life, and breath, and all things;
>
> Act 17:24,25 KJV

My Prayer Journey: Lessons Learned

3 In the summer of 1967, our little congregation composed of our family, the Galbraith's, and a few others, rented a long-empty building that had been erected many years prior as a one-room school house, complete with a bell tower. It was definitely "on the other side of the tracks" near a very poor neighborhood, where even in those years of the 60's, the houses were dirt-floored huts with families that had inter-married and lived in more poverty than I could have ever imagined.

This building was quite large, in comparison to the garage, and was more like a church. It was heated with a gas-burning furnace that sat at the back of the building, probably where a potbellied stove had been in its school house days. We moved our folding chairs from the garage, along with some others that we found or purchased, and moved them in after the old wooden floor had been swept clean and painted shiny and gray. I wonder now if it was left-over paint from the garage floor. In my mind's eye it was the same color, but on wood it didn't seem as cold and shiny as it had on the concrete.

We moved in sometime in May, and our first

service we had the biggest crowd we had ever enjoyed. My aunt and uncle and cousins had come for a visit that week-end and helped fill some of the chairs. It was exciting to have some elbow room after having been in such close quarters. The church yard was shaded by very tall, deciduous trees, probably maple or elm. There was some gravel along-side the church, which had been placed there many years before, as it was only visible through the vegetation if you were standing right on top of it.

It was in this humble, gray-shingle-sided structure that I would earnestly hunger for complete salvation. As the Word was preached and taught, I was fearful of facing the rapture not being filled with the Spirit. There was much teaching about the rapture and the tribulation period that would follow on its heels. This era in earth's existence is a time of God's wrath being poured out, and I did not want to be left to experience the predicted wars and famines, death and destruction. So, I responded to most, if not all, of the altar calls with tears, and trying to give my tongue, the most unruly member of my body (James 3:8), to Jesus. The months passed without the infilling, and the summer ended as I returned to school my 7th-grade year, still lost and undone.

I remember three revival meetings in that building. The one I recall most vividly was that September, as summer's green trees were

My Prayer Journey: Lessons Learned

redecorated in oranges and golds. The evangelists were dear friends of the Galbraith's, Brother and Sister Rodenbush. They were such a handsome, happy, harmonious couple. They preached and sang and loved our little congregation that week without seemingly even noticing our meek surroundings. The Rodenbush's loved God and His Truth and wanted to share it with as many as possible. I recollect Saturday morning, September 30, 1967, that there was a canvassing effort organized. We went to the neighborhood behind the church and invited every family, every child, every passerby to join us the next day in church. Our efforts were rewarded. Along with our tiny congregation and the visitors who responded, we were just one person shy of breaking our attendance record. While Sunday School began and the singing commenced, with our voices chirping out "The Birdie with the Yellow Bill," Bro. Rodenbush slipped out. When he returned, he had two more children in tow and we had the attendance record breakers!

    On Wednesday night of that revival my twin sister, Jean, praying next to me at the altar, received the Holy Ghost. I would become aware of this after I dropped my hands in exhaustion from seeking it myself and smoothed my dress down over my knees. The news hit me hard, and I wondered what she had done to break through that I had not done. I remember feeling more lost than

ever that night on the short-ride home.

Thursday night service came and went, as did Friday and Saturday, and still I had not received the Holy Ghost that I so much desired. After lunch on Sunday, my dad called me to him. As I sat on his lap, he asked, "Do you want the Holy Ghost?" I readily answered, "yes" wondering if I had not made that evident over the years with my multitude trips to the altar. He responded, "Then don't leave that altar tonight until you have it." Something clicked inside me as I slipped down off of his knee that day. Hope sprang afresh and my anticipation began to dance inside as I waited for church time to come. His words had spoken faith in my young heart.

As the preliminary activities drummed slowly by, I could hardly wait for the preaching—and ultimately the invitation—to be given. I can still sense the feeling as I almost skipped down the aisle toward the altar. I would leave here tonight filled to overflowing with the Spirit of God. My accelerated faith and expectation launched me into unrestrained worship and praise for my Savior. The moments that followed will forever be etched in my mind as I heard myself begin to speak words in a language that I did not know. The peace was real. The love enveloped me. I was aware that Sister Rodenbush was praying with me. As I came to the realization of what I had experienced, I felt joy unspeakable well up in my heart. I felt

My Prayer Journey: Lessons Learned

overwhelming, unmistakable love spill over me, and I remember hugging Sister Rodenbush and then running to the piano to hug Sister Galbraith. She had been playing and singing "Won't We Have a Time When We Get Over Yonder," but stopped mid stanza to return my joyous hug. Her eyes danced as she said, "I knew you would get it! It is a promise for everyone!"

Lesson Learned: Seek and you will find.

> And ye shall seek me, and find me, when ye shall search for me with all your heart.
> Jeremiah 29:13 KJV

Notes

My Prayer Journey: Lessons Learned

4 The congregation remained small, with monthly attendance averages in the 30's and 40's. The youth group included my sisters and me and one other girl, Glenda, who lived in another town and did not attend our school. So, Wilmington Jr.- Sr. High had three witnesses to the Truth: the Hoffman girls. We were all good students and had a circle of friends, but we would not make much of an impact witnessing to our peers. The little building we called our church was small and poor compared to the massive St. Rose Catholic limestone church in the center of town, and the large, white-pillared Baptist Church near the entrance to the ranch-house-lined streets of the newer sub-division in Wilmington. Our pride was a problem.

In those days, there were monthly, Monday-night fellowship rallies within the section, and the Galbraith's often took my sisters and me to those meetings. It was always exciting to get to go and see so many people who worshipped and dressed modestly. It was thrilling to see other young people who were living for God and loving it. When choirs from those churches would sing, my eyes would scan every face, lingering on those around

my age as I longed for more Pentecostal friends. But Pastor Galbraith worked a full-time, secular job, and looking back on that now, I understand his sacrifice of time and energy to make sure we attended these meetings. His early morning schedule demanded leaving the services quickly in order to get home and to bed, so there was little opportunity to meet or make new friends.

Lesson Learned: Appreciation for sacrifices made by spiritual leaders.

> Obey them that have the rule over you, and submit yourselves: for they watch for your souls, as they that must give account, that they may do it with joy, and not with grief: for that is unprofitable for you.
>
> Hebrews 13:17 KJV

My Prayer Journey: Lessons Learned

5 I was becoming a teenager and all that goes along with that stage of development: peers, attraction to the opposite sex, and in my world, studying hard to make the grade, preferably A's. In the late 60's and early 70's long hair was in fashion, so that was not a distinguishing factor in blending in with my classmates. However, miniskirts were all the rage, and in order to have a modest length hem, the garment would have to be homemade as the retail racks offered nothing with modesty. Since my mother did not sew, my dresses and skirts were always above my knees and sometimes mid-thigh. My flesh enjoyed not looking too far out of step with my high school girlfriends, yet my newly-filled spirit grieved me over my immodesty.

One Sunday after Sunday School, I remember standing at the end of a row of chairs, when my pastor approached me. I still recall the peach-colored, polyester knit dress that I wore that day. It had a long, pointed, fashionable collar, raised empire waist, and two rows of five white buttons on each side. The hem struck me at least six inches above my knees. As Brother Galbraith stopped,

he very gently and quietly admonished me to lengthen my skirts. It was not a confrontation longer than thirty seconds. His mild manner and kind voice pierced my heart, and the Holy Ghost condemned me. With flushed cheeks and a lump in my throat, I asked the Lord to help me be obedient to his instruction and to find a way to dress more modestly.

Soon it became evident that the Lord had heard my prayers about provision of more modest clothing. Sister Galbraith, Glenda's mom—Honey Lou—(yes that really was her name), and an elderly woman, Sister Quinn, began to sew for me. My mother also took up the challenge and began to create some fashions as well. My wardrobe, slowly but surely, became what was decidedly more acceptable and pleasing to the Lord. Becoming separated from the fashion dictates of the day was both wonderful and horrible. Wonderful in my spirit but sometimes horrifying when secular friends made comments that would embarrass my teenaged emotions. For the most part, though, it felt good in my heart and soul to be pleasing to the Lord in modesty, and it became less awkward around my peers as time passed.

My Prayer Journey: Lessons Learned

Lesson Learned: Obedience may seem impossible, but God makes a way.

And his inward affection is more abundant toward you, whilst he remembereth the obedience of you all, how with fear and trembling ye received him.
2 Corinthians 7:15 KJV

Notes

My Prayer Journey: Lessons Learned

6 In 1971 our congregation was able to purchase another actual church building from the Assembly of God. It was three times the size of the little gray-shingled building, with a small foyer, two nice restrooms and a classroom for Sunday School. The sanctuary had wooden chairs that were connected, five in a section, with fold-up seats. There were three sections of seating with five rows on each side and ten chairs in the middle section. They were painted a neutral, glossy beige which blended with the pale, non-descript, beige-tiled floor. The structure was erected of concrete blocks with a golden-brownish brick facade on the front of the building. The concrete blocks were painted off-white on the inside and behind the pulpit on the front wall hung a 4'x 8' print of Jesus teaching little children. He was dressed in a white garment with a red sash draped across his chest and mid-section. There was a piano sitting on the side of the small platform that also held the pulpit and one row of the five connected chairs. Behind the chairs was a baptismal tank, which was a welcomed sight, since up until now we had literally gone down to the wide Kankakee River to baptize people. This

unassuming, unair-conditioned building was still a big step up from our former habitations. There was a very small rectangular room about 5'x 10' to the side of the platform where I would eventually begin to teach Sunday School. My class of toddlers to age five would be populated with two to five children. There was a small table and chairs that sat in the middle of the room, with four, open, wooden shelves hanging just inside the door to hold my supplies—mainly boxes of eight primary-colored crayons, small plastic scissors, and jars of white paste. I enjoyed the interaction with the sweet-faced children, as even then my storytelling gift began to show itself. There were a few weeks, probably Easter and during summer attendance drives, that I would be required to move the children outside the back door under the massive and messy mulberry tree for our class. Improvising with a well-worn, rag rug, sitting cross-legged and telling stories and singing songs would be the order of the day.

It was during this time that I would begin to communicate on a more personal and consistent level with the Lord. During one of the monthly fellowship meetings, there was an offering being taken for the rather new fund-raising drive, Sheaves for Christ. This offering was an idea of the United Pentecostal Church General Youth Department and has raised millions of dollars to date. It is used to equip our foreign missionaries with vehicles and pays foreign Bible school students' tuition. At the time, in this particular service, I had a five-dollar bill in my purse.

I was working that summer baby-sitting for a family with two, young, unruly boys. From the time they awakened and demanded pancakes for breakfast, until evening, when finally, their parents returned home from work, they kept me on my toes. I watched over these boys from 6AM to 6PM five days a week and was rewarded with twenty dollars. My dad had taught me early to tithe and save on my income. So, after being paid, five dollars would reside in my wallet every week to do whatever I wanted to do with it. There were several things that I could spend my five dollars on. Candy and gum ranked pretty close to the top of my list, but I enjoyed giving and would often save it from week-to-week and buy birthday gifts for my family.

When the offering plea was given, I distinctly heard the Lord ask me for the five dollars I had tucked away in the zippered pocket of my purse. My immediate response was not submissive obedience. My mind cried out, "Are you kidding me!? Not my whole five dollars!" But the Lord gently persisted, and by the time the offering plate passed, I had fingered the folded bill until it was damp and warm but released it in obedience to His request. At that very moment, I felt relief as the offering plate passed on to the end of the pew

and made its way to the front. Obedience felt good and the thought that I, just a mere girl, could be a blessing in the need presented caused my heart to feel happy. I liked the satisfaction that it brought, being a small part of a great need. Five dollars was rather insignificant in comparison to the funds required to meet the need of so many far-off missionaries that I would never meet. Thoughts of the widow woman who gave all she had came to mind, and I made a note to myself to read that Scripture again. Giving, since that experience, has become easy for me.

Soon after that, without request, the father of the rowdy, some days unmanageable boys, gave me twenty-five dollars at the end of the week. When I saw the amount written on the check, my unbelieving eyes lifted back to his face and without hesitation he said, "You earn it." As I walked the half block home that night, I heard Jesus' whisper, "Give and it shall be given unto you."

Hearing His voice ask for my money, and then explaining His precepts of sowing and reaping, made me hungry to converse more with Him.

My Prayer Journey: Lessons Learned

Lesson Learned: You cannot out give God.

Give, and it shall be given unto you; good measure, pressed down, and shaken together, and running over, shall men give into your bosom. For with the same measure that ye mete withal it shall be measured to you again.
Luke 6:38 KJV

Notes

My Prayer Journey: Lessons Learned

7 In the late spring of 1972, I was finishing my junior year of high school. It was an exciting season of life, with new found liberties. Getting a driver's license, having senior "portraits" done, and falling in love with the next-door neighbor boy were the colors of life that surrounded me with shades of the excitement of becoming an adult. I have memories of dreaming what would lie ahead of me; college, marriage, parenthood, and having a home of my own floated in and out of my adolescent mind.

One particular night I went to an Illinois District, Section 10, Sheaves for Christ Youth Rally with my pastor and his wife. The meeting was in Lockport, Illinois, and the crowd was large in comparison to our little group in Wilmington. The size of the congregation always made this young girl excited, seeing many conservatively dressed young people that loved to worship God unreservedly. The air was super-charged with the presence of God, and the wonderful praise and worship that opened the service swept me away into the keen awareness of the presence of my loving Savior. I still recall sitting on the side aisle, second row pew, with my hands uplifted and

tears trickling downward as I enjoyed His sweet presence. The Scripture text came to mind, "When I consider thy heavens, and the work of thy fingers, the moon and the stars, which thou hast ordained; What is man, that thou are mindful of him?" I recall feeling enveloped in His arms and exploring Him on a more personal level as I worshipped that night.

The service progressed, the preacher preached, the choir sang, and the altar call was given. The crowded church left little room at the altar, and so without too much choice I knelt at that second-row pew and began to pray. The pew was upholstered with durable, red material, and as I buried my young face into my hands and the burlap-like fabric imprinted itself onto the back of my hands, I heard from the Lord again. His still small voice boomed into my brain, instructing me of the work he was calling me for and that I would need to prepare myself by attending Apostolic Bible Institute in St. Paul, Minnesota. I tried to digest what He was saying to me, attempting to push down the fear of the unknown. He gently but firmly pushed the issue and asked me for a commitment to follow His bidding. After more than three-quarters of an hour of pleading prayer, I submitted. Again, as I arose from my altar, I felt the refreshing relief that comes with obedience to your Creator.

My Prayer Journey: Lessons Learned

Lesson Learned: Obedience is better than sacrifice.

> And Samuel said, Hath the LORD as great delight in burnt offerings and sacrifices, as in obeying the voice of the LORD? Behold, to obey is better than sacrifice…
>
> 1 Samuel 15:22a KJV

Notes

My Prayer Journey: Lessons Learned

8 As my high school senior year dawned, I was returning to school with the experience of hearing God's voice, responding to Him, and enjoying the peace of obeying. I remember, during that fall season, being called to a more consistent time of prayer. My Bible became more prominent in my day's schedule, and I would often pray for direction as I read it. It was during that warm autumn that I would choose and memorize Psalm 46:1, "God is our refuge and strength, a very present help in trouble" as my "life's Scripture." I could not realize how many times in the coming years that I would run to that Scripture for comfort and encouragement.

My memories of that year are filled with excitement as I prepared to be obedient and make plans to go to Apostolic Bible Institute. In my free time, I would pour over the college catalog and year book. I would dream of meeting the people represented by their yearbook portraits and imagine becoming friends with this college world. I would dream of the beautiful, huge, 600-seat United Pentecostal Church auditorium and what I would learn, feel, and become once I reached that place. Freshman orientation, Leaf Day, a day spent in a local park picnicking and playing sports when the colors were at their peak, Christmas banquets, and end-of-the-year class dramas enthralled me. I knew, in my core, that God had a plan for me, and it would take a more definitive form once I arrived in this far-off city. Until then my life was spent in a rural and small-town atmosphere, and I had no idea what this metropolitan area would be like.

My prayer life during those days became full of anticipation as I poured out my intentions to obey His call. Yet it was still a before meal, church-service-centered existence, but it was these prayer times that began to shape me into the person that I am today. I would realize while standing in the altar or kneeling at my pew that God was more than a story.

Lesson Learned: God has a personal plan for my life.

> For I know the thoughts that I think toward you, saith the LORD, thoughts of peace, and not of evil, to give you an expected end.
> Jeremiah 29:11 KJV

My Prayer Journey: Lessons Learned

9 June 1973 arrived with hot weather, caps and gowns, and good-byes to classmates. I worked in the high school guidance office throughout my senior year and stayed on through the summer saving every penny in preparation for college. My dad was not thrilled with my plan of going to a non-accredited Bible college. He would talk to me about the practicality of living at home and enrolling in Joliet Junior College to gain credits toward a degree that would be useful in my life. "I will help finance Joliet Junior, but you will be on your own if you pursue this Christian education that will not benefit your future." My personality type is 'people-pleasing' and to buck my beloved dad was not something I had ever done. I remember going to my room after that conversation and sitting on my bed praying, "God, was that really You? Your Word tells me to obey my parents, so what should I do?" It was during this period of time that I began to fast along with my prayers. My increasingly prioritized prayer, coupled with fasting, empowered me with courage and peace about my future and where it was taking me.

As the summer unfolded, I felt confirmed in my decision to follow through with the plan. One day, mid-summer, I quietly but firmly told my dad of my intentions and asked him for his blessings. He never verbalized his agreement but from that time on made travel plans to take me to ABI for the beginning of my freshman year. He would never finance my decision but would support me with visits, calls, and prayer. I managed to save about 600 dollars by summer's end.

I had enjoyed a 'friendship-turned-romance' over the summer prior to graduation and throughout that school year. Bill lived next door and was a mild-mannered, fun-loving, sports-minded boy. We enjoyed golf, which was in actuality, him playing and me watching. Dairy Queen was our favorite. We also spent time sitting in our adjoining back yards under dozens of tall oak trees. Our lockers were situated closely, he carried my books, made me laugh, and was a gentleman. He visited our church a couple of times but was a member at a country Methodist church down the road. Once during our "Youth Week" he came to hear me speak on my topic "This Little Light of Mine." I demonstrated the power of the flame of one candle in a darkened room and pointed out the impact we, as Christians, are called to make in the dark world.

As the summer was concluding, Bill stopped by one evening and invited me to take a walk with

My Prayer Journey: Lessons Learned

him. Hand-in-hand we strolled down two blocks to the Kankakee River that flowed through our little town. As the evening was closing in and the river rushed by, we talked about our future. He asked me not to go to ABI. He wanted me to stay and enroll in Joliet Junior College with him, and for the first time in our relationship told me that he loved me and wanted our future to be shared. This hurdle proved to be one last obstacle to test my commitment to obedience. I had confirmed in my heart after the confrontation with my dad that I would follow the leading of the Lord. Although I shared emotional ties with this high school beau, I knew in the moment that I must pursue God's plan. We agreed to stay the course and not correspond. If we were truly in love, then absence would make the heart grow fonder. If our future was not to be shared, then the other cliché, 'out of sight out of mind,' would soon become evident. We both cried walking home that night, but I knew in my heart that the chapter was closing on this sweet, youthful relationship.

    The buzzing of the travel alarm clock awakened me in the pre-dawn hours that late August morning. The day had come! I was on my way to taking my first step to the rest of my life. A hurried prayer of thanksgiving and request for safe travels and courage to complete this day breezed through my consciousness. I had bid my sisters and grandmother good-bye the night before. The car was packed and my dad's coffee thermos was full of steaming dark brew as we crept quietly out to the garage. The backwards glance into my home and the quick petting of my sweet dog, Candy, brought the ever- too-familiar lump in my throat. Tears threatened to spill from my eyes as I took this huge leap into the unknown.

As I got into the back seat of my parents 1969, green, Chevy station wagon, the Lord got in with me. His reassurances filled my mind. In those early morning hours, the dark-olive, vinyl seat became my altar and brought the calm assurance that this was the day the Lord had made, and I would rejoice and be glad in it.

Lesson Learned: Obedience means stepping out by faith.

> For we walk by faith, not by sight;
> 2 Corinthians 5:7 KJV

My Prayer Journey: Lessons Learned

10

We arrived in St. Paul late in the afternoon. Entering the lobby, as unfamiliar faces swarmed around the ABI office counter, I stood back with questions that come with new and strange environments. "Had I really heard from God?" "Was I really supposed to be doing this?" "Why would God want me here without my twin sister?" "What am I doing here?" My anxiety was quickly turning into panic, when the kind lady behind the desk motioned me forward. She indeed found my name on her list and quickly began calculating my first semester's matriculation fees, charges, and room and board for the first three weeks, due immediately. My checkbook was drained, but I was good for three weeks. From there my parents took me to the dorm where I would be housed for the next two years. The enrollment that year was the largest in the history of the school. Due to my last-minute arrival, I was assigned to what had been the 'rec room' the year before. The room had quickly been vacated of ping pong tables, card tables and the like, and had been transformed into a dormitory room with four bunk beds and dressers. 'Overwhelmed,' 'scared,' and 'disappointed' are mild descriptions compared to the emotions that filled my being, and once again the questions emerged. My parents had carried in my lone suitcase along with my garment bag and two boxes of personal items. It did not take long to unpack those few belongings. The dark evening was closing in, and my parents were needing to find a hotel for the night. As their car made the curve around the road, and their glowing red tail lights disappeared, I felt so alone. I gave in to the feelings of separation from all that was familiar, and wept.

As I tentatively made my way back into the dorm, I felt overwhelmed with loneliness in the biggest city I would ever call home. I was homesick for my three sisters in a room full of eight new dorm mates. I asked the Lord to help me find a friend. He replied, "I will never leave you or forsake you." My mental response was "I appreciate that, Lord, but I really need a friend I can see tonight." The seven other girls in the room and I had won the same lottery in this recreation room turned home. They were mulling around unpacking, laughing, and seemed to be enjoying themselves. I was awash in fear of the unknown and feelings of homesickness. "Oh no! What had I done?!" As I crawled up to the top bunk that fell my lot, I turned my back on the room, closed my

My Prayer Journey: Lessons Learned

eyes, and swallowed back the pain of a throat lump that felt boulder-sized. "How could I do this?" Before sleep overtook me, I breathed a silent prayer into my tear-soaked pillow, "You are going to have to help me here." God's reply was once again, "I will never leave you or forsake you."

The beginning of classes, homework assignments, job searches, and daily class schedules filled my awake time. These dynamics began to overtake and diminish the ache in the center of my being. The classes were engaging and enthralling. His Word became alive. The invitation by the Spirit drew me to a room designated for prayer where there were kneeling benches covered in aqua carpet attached to rough paneled walls. It was in this room, and at this time in my life, that I established a daily, regular time with my Savior. It was here that I realized He was in control, ordering my steps, and revealing yet unrevealed truths in my life. He assured me that He would love me, guide me, and provide for me.

During those weeks, I became friends with Debbie. She had a car, I did not. She had family in the area, I did not. She had worked as a waitress, I had not. It was through this relationship that the Lord provided a job, transportation, and the money to support my freshman year. A Sambo's Family Restaurant was opening on White Bear Avenue, a 20-minute drive from the college. The manager took a special liking to Debbie and I and would schedule us together when it was an option. In my red aproned pockets, I would carry home my tips: quarters, dimes, and nickels, and dump them into a little cedar box. Every Friday I would carry that little box to the business office and count enough coins to pay for my room and board for the week. I am convinced the box was often like the widow's cruse; there was always just enough.

Lesson Learned: He will always be my Friend, never leaving me or forsaking me.

> …for he hath said, I will never leave thee, nor forsake thee.
>
> Hebrews 13:5 KJV

My Prayer Journey: Lessons Learned

11

During my freshman and sophomore years at Bible College I was learning more from the Word of God, as most classes were centered there. I was praying regularly in the prayer room and during class-called prayer meetings. The church services were full of deep, reserved worship, less exuberant than what I had been accustomed to. This dynamic was judged by some as less spiritual, but on the contrary, I found a new depth in my relationship with the Lord and a new sensitivity to His voice. The 600-member congregation, deeply rooted in Scandinavian reservation, was genuine in their generational commitments to the Apostolic message of the Mighty God in Christ, the salvation plan presented in the book of Acts, and modesty of dress and conduct.

The end-of-service altar calls regularly found me on the left side of the 4-foot-high platform bottom step, soaking the carpet with tears. Tears of joy, tears of repentance, and tears of commitment flowed often and long in these college days. It was there, during a school devotion turned altar service, that I cried out to my God for my father.

My dad was a hard-working, family-leading provider and protector. He had been filled with the Holy Ghost and baptized in Jesus' Name early in my parent's marriage but had never fully submitted himself to the leading of the Spirit. He was my hero even though at this time in his life he was not deacon material. He had an addiction to nicotine since its introduction into his life at the age of thirteen. He had a quick temper which could be vocalized in words that we, his girls, were not allowed to use. He never opposed our church attendance and indeed attended himself as often as his rotating shift work allowed. He paid his tithes, joined in at work day maintenance at the church, and gave Christmas gifts to the pastor's family. I adored him. I had learned during my once-a-week call from home, early on Sunday mornings, that he had been diagnosed with stomach ulcers. He was experiencing a great deal of pain.

As I began to weep with concern and fear for his physical and spiritual health, I began to intercede with groanings and finally in tongues for his healing. During that service, one of the leaders said from the pulpit that if we were praying for someone with physical ailments, we were to bring something forward—a handkerchief or some kind of object that could be anointed, prayed over, and sent to the person in need. I immediately wanted to comply but had nothing that I could take. I

My Prayer Journey: Lessons Learned

remember folding a tear-stained tissue into a two-inch square and making my way up the stairs to the podium. Several ministers and students prayed with me for my dad.

I wrote dad a letter and explained what had happened to me that day during prayer time. I enclosed the tissue anointed with prayer, tears, and anointing oil, and mailed it off.

The next time I was with my dad, he opened his wallet and revealed the prayer cloth. He looked into my eyes and told me he had felt no pain since receiving it. He carried that tissue for years after that in his wallet. He showed it to me several times. To my knowledge he never had any other stomach issues.

During this time period, we started to notice a change in dad spiritually as well. He continued to work for ten more years, and the day he retired from Amoco Chemicals, he laid down his pipe, cold turkey, at the age of fifty-six. He was noticeably less quick to respond in anger, and I don't remember a curse word for many years before he passed away suddenly from the effects of a stroke at the age of 81.

Lesson learned: God hears the cries of our hearts.

Hear my cry, O God; attend unto my prayer.
Psalm 61:1 KJV

Notes

My Prayer Journey: Lessons Learned

12 At eighteen years and some months, I was getting to know Jesus, His Word, and His voice in a deeper way every day. I had been assigned a ten-minute devotion for my public speaking class. I was energized by the thought, as I had enjoyed giving oral book reports in elementary school, playing parts in plays that my sisters and cousins and I would put together, and teaching my Sunday School classes.

I began to pray that the Lord would speak to me and through me and that I could communicate it in a way that would be meaningful to me and to others. As my prayer and daily Bible reading continued, the Lord's voice became more distinct. One cold and snowy Minnesota afternoon, He spoke to me, "Your life is a story being told." It was a concept I had not previously known, but in those moments, I knew Who I wanted to author my life's story. "...we spend our years as a tale that is told" (Psalms 90:9). I used this Scripture for my text reference as I spoke to my classmates that day.

The idea that He had planted in my mind that day has been a perennial flower in the garden of my heart. Seasons have come and seasons have gone, but the notion that my life was a story, that I needed God to be the author, and that it would require my purposeful submission, was clear.

The memory of His voice directing me to give, to go to ABI, and now to assign the writing of my story to Him was causing great joy and excitement in me. Watching Him order my steps and my thoughts was thrilling. I wanted more and more to hear, comprehend, and obey.

It was during this time that I went to bed one night, falling onto my bunk in exhaustion. Being a full-time student and working thirty hours a week as a waitress was starting to tell in my energy levels. I remember turning my bedside light off and turning my back on my roommates who were still milling around in the room. As the room quieted, I fell into a much-needed deep sleep. Hours later I awakened in cave-like darkness with the sensation of being weighted down in a paralyzed, all-encompassing fear. I heard demon-like laughter and taunts from spiritual beings that could only be evil. I could not move. I could not speak. I was drenched in sweat and the terror was all consuming. In those moments I heard the voice I was learning to recognize. "Call out My name, I am here, call on Me."

My mouth was cotton-like-dry, and my lips were tingling and unresponsive. Repeatedly I tried to say "Jesus," but could not get it out. The

My Prayer Journey: Lessons Learned

weights on my chest and abdomen were choking me. I couldn't breathe or speak. Finally, a hoarse whisper escaped my lips, "Jesus." Then a less subdued, "Jesus." And finally, I shouted "Jesus!"

The weight lifted, I could breathe, and the blackness became the darkness of my dorm room sprinkled with the illumination of several night lights. I had heard voices, inaudible but palpable voices of dread, fear, and darkness trying to overtake me—then the 'Voice' of love and light. That merciful, loving voice spoke reassurances that He was victorious over the spirits I had encountered that long-ago night.

Getting up from my bunk, I padded to the pay phone in the hallway and dropped my dime in the slot. I called my friend, Mark, who would eighteen months later become my husband. I related the entire experience to him. He heard the panic in my voice and prayed with me to understand what had happened and to learn the lesson that had just been taught.

Lesson Learned: Going deeper in the Lord will be challenged by the enemy of our souls. Jesus is victorious!

> Submit yourselves therefore to God. Resist the devil, and he will flee from you.
> James 4:7 KJV

Notes

My Prayer Journey: Lessons Learned

13

As weeks turned into months, I was spending more time in the Word than ever before. I was learning to read the Bible with understanding. Before, I would read the words and concentrate on the stories, but now I was realizing the inspiration of the Book and that it was truly alive. This best seller of all time had purpose, holding the answers to all my questions.

I had worked a long shift at my waitressing job and had returned to my dorm room, pulling on a thick robe and knee socks to try and fight off the chill of that Minnesota late November night. I climbed up onto my top bunk, grabbed my Bible, and began to read in the gospel of John. In the beginning was the Word… hey, wait a minute… that's how Genesis starts! Flipping to the front I read, "In the beginning God." Wow! My pulse quickened as the God of creation began to speak to me with words of instruction and revelation. I quickly flipped back to John and read chapter one, verses one through fourteen, and again the prickly warm sensation of His nearness washed over me. "…the Word was made flesh and dwelt among us!"

A light bulb moment that I will never forget happened to me as I sat cradling my Bible in my cross-legged lap that night. I had been taught the doctrine of the Oneness of God all of my Pentecostal life, but in that one moment God Almighty, the Creator of the heavens and earth, revealed to me that He robed Himself in flesh and came to earth to walk among mankind to be the Lamb slain before the foundation of the world.

I will always cherish that evening that drew me closer to the Mighty God in Christ. My prayer life changed after that revelation. He was becoming my personal Friend. He would speak to me, Jane Hoffman, an 18-year-old, middle class girl from a midwestern dot on the map—a human. He was gently leading me into a loving relationship through my commitment to prayer and Bible study.

Exposure to these disciplines held great possibilities. His Word would become a lamp unto my feet. His Word would speak to me and show me things I could not know without hearing from Him. He would give me ears to hear what thus saith the Lord! (Matthew 11:15)

My Prayer Journey: Lessons Learned

Lesson learned: He wants to have a dialogue with me.

Moreover, he said unto me, Son of man, all my words that I shall speak unto thee receive in thine heart, and hear with thine ears.
Ezekiel 3:10 KJV

Notes

My Prayer Journey: Lessons Learned

14

As the appointed three years of my ABI chapter was drawing to a close, I was to face some uncertainties that brought anxiety. Mark and I married at the close of our junior year and would be married students for the next 12 months. Although this new relationship was filled with fun and enjoyment, it was a time with new schedule demands. Moving into off-campus housing, maintaining our classes, working as full-time employees, and now adding the responsibilities of a marriage relationship caused our plates to be full and running over. My husband was returned to the office of class president and I as class treasurer. These offices had requirements of leadership that often caused our exhaustion to push past human limits.

Withstanding so many pressures and enjoying a steady and fruitful prayer life was nearly impossible. We prayed regularly before our meals, before each class period, and in church services. We were studying His Word, typing class assignments, leading class meetings and raising funds, working our secular jobs, and paying the bills. Besides all of this, we were staring down the barrel of our future and wanting desperately to have our steps ordered by the Lord.

I was missing my old dormitory prayer room where I had put down roots in a land of growing my relationship with Him. Where could I be alone anymore? The three-room apartment did not offer any place of solitude to seek His face. As I looked for the opportunity, and tried to fall into another place of routine, I found that my commute to downtown St. Paul six days a week was the place and time to be with Jesus. He rode with me on those miles every day, but I was unaware of His presence in the passenger seat until I longed for private time with Him. It was during those drives that I learned how much He loved for me to sing to Him. My singing voice is mediocre at best, but He never seems to notice flat notes or poor timing. The songs would flow from my heart, and He would respond quickly to these heart songs. During that era, we listened to LP records from emerging United Pentecostal Church artists and Bible school choirs. The lyrics were soul-touching and worship-inducing. I learned that listening to heartfelt music could be another way to commune with the Lover of my soul. As I sang to Him, He would embrace me and assure me that He was interested in me and would never leave me.

On those commutes, once in His Presence, I pondered several opportunities that had been

My Prayer Journey: Lessons Learned

offered to us upon graduation. There were two offers that came from our home churches, from our pastors, whom we loved and respected. These opportunities were attractive to us, meaning that we would be near family and in familiar places. But in April 1976, before graduation later that year, an offer and proposal came from a former Bible School instructor, whom we admired. He pastored a small congregation of approximately eighty parishioners in Bourbon, Indiana. The opportunity brought great anticipation for both my husband and me. My husband would be the assistant pastor, and we would both serve as youth leaders.

Singing "Only Jesus Can Satisfy Your Soul" while driving in four lanes of construction traffic, Jesus whispered, "I will satisfy your longings in Bourbon." His assurances came to me, and even today He is the only true satisfaction of my heart.

Lesson learned: He will meet me wherever I am.

> The LORD thy God in the midst of thee is mighty; he will save, he will rejoice over thee with joy; he will rest in his love, he will joy over thee with singing.
>
> Zephaniah 3:17 KJV

Notes

My Prayer Journey: Lessons Learned

15

Graduation had come and gone. We had taken another leap of faith into the abyss of the unknown. Mark and I had accepted the offer and moved to Bourbon for him to serve in the United Pentecostal Church there. We found ourselves moving into a small, second-floor, one-bedroom apartment filled with the warmth and humidity of Indiana summers. A small window air conditioner hummed away, trying to keep up. It was June 28, 1976, our first wedding anniversary. As I crawled out of bed and padded to the kitchen, the worries of the day quickly descended. He had left earlier for the first day of his new secular job in a small wire factory. It would be two weeks before we would hold a pay check in our hands. I had yet to find employment. I picked up the bills from the small dinette table and thumbed through them. Mark and I had talked about it the evening before and acknowledged that there were no funds to pay any of them.

I carried them down the hall to the living room and laid them out one by one on the green velour couch cushions. As I knelt, I began to report to the Lord as if He was completely unaware of our dire circumstances. "Lord, we have been obedient and moved here to work for you. We have always paid our tithes and given extra offerings when we could. I don't have any ideas about these bills, Lord, but we don't want a blot on our reputation by letting them be late or unpaid." I whined on and on about His promises to provide and quoted Scripture about opening the windows of heaven and pouring out blessings.

As I continued praying, I had just picked up the last invoice, when I heard the clink of the mailbox as the mail carrier dropped in our mail. I stood up, running my hands through my hair and wiping my eyes, and headed down the steep flight of stairs. As I got to the bottom of the steps, I noticed that the lid of the mailbox was propped open with several envelopes. I grabbed them and started flipping through them as I turned to ascend the stairs. No more bills, thank you, Jesus. A card from my mom and dad who were living in Spain for the summer, a card from a former boss of my husband at 3M in St. Paul, an official looking envelope from the State of Minnesota.

Sitting down on the couch, next to my pile of impossibilities, I began to open my mail. An anniversary card from my mom and dad with a check enclosed. This was not unusual, but the timing, coming from Spain, on this particular morning was excellent. Thank you, Jesus! The next card was also an anniversary card. There was

My Prayer Journey: Lessons Learned

something extremely unusual about this one. The sender was a middle-aged man who himself had never been married, but was thoughtful enough to remember us—with a check enclosed! Thank you, Jesus! Finally, the scary looking letter from the State of Minnesota. With a bit of trepidation, I slit open the envelope. To my great delight it was a totally unexpected refund check for overpaid taxes. There was an explanation of a mistake we had made when filing that was noticed.

As I grabbed a pen and pad to add up our windfall, I began to whoop for joy. The total would not only pay the bills I had stacked next to me, but after tithing, there was still 20 dollars left to enjoy a restaurant meal for our anniversary. Jehovah Jireh, my provider.

Lesson Learned: He provides.

> Behold the fowls of the air: for they sow not, neither do they reap, nor gather into barns; yet your heavenly Father feedeth them. Are ye not much better than they?
>
> Matthew 6:26 KJV

Notes

My Prayer Journey: Lessons Learned

16

One blustery November night in 1979, my husband had left our home to go pray at the church. After three and a half years in Bourbon, we had been feeling the uneasiness that comes when some kind of change is ahead but not knowing what the change will be. It is a la-la land of sorts that causes you to seek direction. Mark was feeling the nudge to take another step in the ministry. We had loved our time there and learned a lot. The thought of being a pastor's wife set a deep cold chill in my weak backbone. I knew as pastor and wife the 'buck would stop here.' I thought it a much more pleasant scenario to leave the conflict and battles to someone else and make an exit with a pat on the back and the encouragement, "We'll be praying for you."

As the praying continued about our future, I started naively telling God my set of requirements and stipulations for me to be willing to become a pastoring couple. For me to move into the role of pastor's wife, I felt that it would have to be an established church of seventy-five or more. The church needed to have a parsonage, as we were as poor as paupers, and to put the icing on the cake, Mark needed to be full time. Oh, and it needed to be in Illinois near my parents. My mantra for several weeks was, "So God, let me know when you have that place prepared, and I will be glad to try to do Your will."

That particular night, after Mark left, I put Matthew, our one-year-old son, to bed and found an altar on the floor by the same green living room sofa where I had learned He would be my provider. I again started down my long list of requirements if He wanted me to be a pastor's wife. He interrupted tenderly with an "excuse me?" Even though He was gentle, I felt the rebuke and fell silent. Before I got up from prayer, the couch was soaked with repentant tears, and there were used tissues strewn around my knees. My absolute obedience to His request had been obtained in that prayer meeting. I would go wherever He was calling my husband, with the knowledge that He would not lead us anywhere that He was not going along.

Lesson learned: It's about Him and His plan, not about me and my desires.

> Commit thy works unto the LORD, and thy thoughts shall be established.
>
> Proverbs 16:3 KJV

My Prayer Journey: Lessons Learned

17

Just days later, after my submission to the Lord's leading, we were on our way to meet with a small group of people in Bucyrus, Ohio. While my husband had been praying at the church that night, there was a call to our pastor from a man who had been shepherding this small group of people. He was leaving for a call to Tanzania, Africa. He was needing someone to turn his little flock over to. Even though Mark had been born and raised in Columbus, Ohio, he had never heard of Bucyrus. It was a small town of about 13,000 people, an hour north of Columbus, where Mark's family still lived.

I remember driving into a well-groomed town on Route 30. We passed by the Brown Derby Restaurant, the Holiday Inn, a small hospital, more restaurants, and some businesses. It seemed 'nice.' The church was meeting once a week in a small meeting room at the City Town Hall building at 2:30 on Sunday afternoons. There was a keyboard being played by the soon-to-be absent missionary's wife. I didn't play. When it came time for the offering, a repurposed, Cool Whip tub was passed around. During my husband's sermon, the earnest people leaned in and accepted the Word with eagerness. And so, just days later, we accepted the position as pastor with this little fledgling group of people. We packed up our little family of three in a truck owned by one of the parishioners in Bourbon and headed east.

Some of the people in Bucyrus would endear themselves to us in ways that would impact us for the rest of our lives. The stories we lived out there are life lessons, adventures, and experiences that are repeated many times over when talking about "the good old days" with family and friends.

There was nothing impressive by the world's standards. Certainly, nothing on my list of prerequisites were met in Bucyrus. But it felt right. It would be here in this little city that Mark and I would find Jesus to be our constant Friend and Provider. It would be in this location that our second son, Nathan, would be born. And it would be in Bucyrus where I would learn new ways to pray and intercede.

Lesson Learned: God's ways are not our ways. His thoughts, not our thoughts.

> For as the heavens are higher than the earth, so are my ways higher than your ways, and my thoughts than your thoughts.
>
> Isaiah 55:9 KJV

My Prayer Journey: Lessons Learned

18

My boys were tucked in for the night. The chirping of crickets could be heard through the second story opened windows. The leaves in the maple tree were rustling in the warm summer breeze. As I laid down on our bed and sighed with the tiredness of the day, I was feeling lonely for my husband. He was away for a week, selling insurance door to door, trying to make ends meet. I began to pray, but before long my sleepiness won the battle and I drifted off. I began to breathe the slow steady breath of sleep.

About two hours later I was awakened by the doorbell ringing. Ding-dong. Ding-dong. Ding-dong. Someone was urgently trying to awaken me. Grabbing my robe, I ran down the stairs to see who it was. Before I could get to the door, the person began beating on the door and saying, "Let me in!"

Flipping on the porch light, I could see a man standing just on the other side of the oval window in the Victorian door. He had opened the storm door and was now beating on the glass with his fists, saying he was coming in and he knew I was alone. He threatened vulgarities and was rattling the door handle.

With my heart racing, I flipped off the light and started running back upstairs. I tripped over the coffee table and fell hard, banging my knee. The pain shot thru my leg, and hot tears stung my eyes as I got up to continue trying to get away from the monster outside the door. He was still banging and swearing as I reached the upstairs hallway. I grabbed my boys out of their beds, ran to my room and flipped the hook and eye closure lock in place. Somehow the boys never stirred. I placed them on the bed, grabbed the rotary dial phone to call the police but did not know the number. This was before the days of 911. So, I called the first number that came to mind—some dear friends that lived ten miles from town. Trying to communicate my plight, my friends understood that I was in trouble. They told me to hang up, stay in my room, and they would call the police and be on their way.

About that time, silence became louder than the screaming, and I feared the intruder had gotten in the house and was coming for us. I kept listening for creaks on the steps, but none came.

It seemed like forever, but I finally heard sirens coming and saw red lights flashing. When the police arrived, they found the drunken man passed out on our porch. Our friends, Jack and Marilyn, soon followed. When they saw who the man was, they recognized him as a visitor to our church

My Prayer Journey: Lessons Learned

service the Sunday before. My pastor husband had made a public announcement to our small congregation that he would be out of town that week and if anyone needed anything they could contact me.

Lesson Learned: Even when I fail to pray, He protects me.

> For I the LORD thy God will hold thy right hand, saying unto thee, Fear not; I will help thee.
>
> Isaiah 41:13 KJV

Notes

My Prayer Journey: Lessons Learned

19

Mark returned, and normal life resumed. Supper one night would be an easy preparation. The only thing I had on the shelf was a can of corn and our last box of eleven cent macaroni and cheese. As I opened the can, pouring the yellow kernels into a sauce pan and ripping open the cardboard box, my thoughts were on the next day's meal. I wondered what I would do when my growing boys expected breakfast, let alone lunch and dinner. I began to pray under my breath, "God, I know You will provide. I don't know how, but I know, You will."

It was a dark evening in the shortness of a November day. I remember looking out the dining room window as the wind blew the dark arthritic fingers of the old maple tree branches against the side of the house. Snow flurries had begun to fall and my heart was beginning to feel dismal. Although my prayer declared faith, my heart began to worry.

The boys were playing at my feet. Although we had a generic brand macaroni and cheese often, indeed sometimes for two meals a day, they still miraculously danced with delight when it was on the menu. "Yeah, macaroni and cheese!" I often wondered, during those days, if the children in the wilderness loved manna as much as my boys loved this bright colored pasta.

 I called my husband to the table, and as he saw both serving bowls filled with yellow, he glanced in my direction with raised eyebrows. His unspoken words were answered with my non-verbal reply, and he understood that we had reached the end of our groceries. He slumped into his chair feeling the weight of provision. I knew he, too, was praying a prayer of hope for the next day's meals.

 As we joined hands in thanks, the doorbell rang. I opened the door to a dear elderly sister from our church. As she stood in the coldness of the night, her headscarf tied tightly under her chin, she asked if I could help her get something out of her car. Grabbing a sweater from the peg, I ran down the porch steps to her car parked on the street. As she opened the trunk, the contents were packed tightly into big brown grocery bags and boxes. I sucked in wonderful relief as she excitedly told me, "I was going into the grocery store to shop when the Lord told me I needed to be shopping for the pastor's family! So, I just went up and down those aisles grabbing whatever He had on the list!"

 There were cases of canned fruits and vegetables, bags of pastas and sauces, cereal, meat, dairy products, and even laundry soaps. It

My Prayer Journey: Lessons Learned

was more food than we had in our home for a long time.

I went to bed that night with a sweet satisfaction that the Lord did know where we were and that He was going to provide.

Lesson Learned: He is always on time.

> The LORD is good unto them that wait for him, to the soul that seeketh him. It is good that a man should both hope and quietly wait for the salvation of the LORD.
>
> Lamentations 3:25-26 KJV

Notes

My Prayer Journey: Lessons Learned

20

It had been "the best of times;" it had been "the worst of times." We had been blessed with our second son, happy and healthy. The church was growing, we were teaching Home Bible Studies. The Christian Apostolic Church of Bucyrus, Ohio, was now meeting in her own, howbeit small and basic, building. The loan had been procured with a monthly payment of $212. The utilities were doable. There was enough in the checking account to make ends meet, even with paying my pastor husband $50 weekly. Those were lean times, but God was providing.

We were making ends meet with tedious stretching of our resources. As the church grew, we cultivated a widening circle of friends and acquaintances, but there were days and weeks that loneliness would set in like a dark thunderhead on a bright sunny day. We had little or no contact with friends in the ministry. It often seemed as if we were fighting, struggling, barely keeping our heads above the water, and alone.

It was one such night when my husband and I sat in the dark on the couch. The boys were asleep.

We were both silent. Our moods were dark. Did anyone at all know where we were? Or worse, did anyone care? We needed a word from the Lord, an encouraging phone call, even a card in the mail with a ten-dollar bill inside would have made us feel so much better. But no card came, the phone didn't ring, and the skies were silent.

Our thoughts raged. We silently sought relief. "God are You out there?! Don't You see how lonely we are?! Can't You send someone, anyone, to care about us?!

Brrrrinnnnng. Suddenly the phone on the kitchen wall was ringing.

Shocked, we looked at each other and lunged for the phone. My husband got there first. "Hello?" The voice on the other end was a gentleman from the church we had left in Indiana. Though not in formal ministry, he was a spiritually sensitive man that the Lord was using in that very moment. The conversation lasted less than ten minutes, but the message of love resonates in our hearts yet today. He had been praying and God had shown him our faces. He is typically a man of few words. He wanted us to know that we were remembered and loved. He also said that he knew God was with us and for us. His call was inspired by the Lord, right at that very moment, in our hour of despair.

My Prayer Journey: Lessons Learned

Lesson Learned: God is always there, no matter how lonely you may feel.

Be strong and of a good courage, fear not, nor be afraid of them: for the LORD thy God, he it is that doth go with thee; he will not fail thee, nor forsake thee.
Deuteronomy 31:6 KJV

Notes

My Prayer Journey: Lessons Learned

21

Matt was six. Our normally bouncing-off-the-walls, hopping, skipping, singing, happy boy was burning up with fever. He said his stomach hurt. He was lethargic. Not having medical insurance and treating the symptoms, we prayed and believed it was a 'bug' and he would be better in a couple of days. Day three he was not better. In fact, his temperature was rising. So, we called Dr. Lyons, our family doctor, and reported the symptoms. We were instructed to go to the emergency room and he would meet us there. He suspected a ruptured appendix.

After an exam and bloodwork results, the supposed appendicitis was ruled out. We started down the path to diagnosis with ultrasounds, more labs, and consults. After a couple of agonizing days in the hospital, where they packed his little body in ice blankets to bring down the fever, we were sent to another hospital to be seen by a specialist. More exams, tests, and finally CT-scans were done.

We were called into an office to be gently informed, "We found a tumor on Matt's left kidney the size of a grapefruit. Prepare yourselves for the worst." We were in shock. The doctor showed us the protrusion on his back where the tumor was. How had I missed that? It was obviously swollen. I think about it now and understand that at that point, I was running the bath water, and Matt was getting himself undressed, into the tub, drying himself off, and putting on his own pajamas. So, there would have been no reason for me to notice it without any complaints of discomfort from him. But in the moment, I felt like the worst mother ever. The emotions of caring for our very sick child, wondering what was going to happen next, and the worry of rising bills had taken its toll. Mark and I stared at the doctor totally speechless. "What do you mean, prepare for the worst?" Our little boy was a healthy, happy, energetic kid who had never been sick. Other than the regular childhood ailments and allergies, he was fine! My maternal heart cracked that day when I heard those words. After the report sunk in, all I could do was say, "Please, Jesus!"

By this time, Matt had been in the hospital for ten days. He was barely eating anything. IVs were keeping him hydrated. He was a very sick, little boy. The specialist told us he wanted to do surgery to see if the tumor could be removed. After that, he would be able to decide what kind of treatment would be necessary. He said he may need to remove the tumor, along with the kidney, once he was able to visualize the growth.

My Prayer Journey: Lessons Learned

We cried, we stared into space, and relied on others to pray. We were numb.

Early the next morning we were standing at Matt's bedside awaiting the surgical team to take our seriously ill little boy away. The surgeon entered the room and explained to us that he had been awake most of the night preparing for the surgery, thinking about Matt, and praying. He then asked us if we would consent to another CT-scan before he made the incision. He explained that he wanted to compare the images to see how much the tumor had grown since the last scan. We signed the consent document and Matt was wheeled down the corridor to x-ray. About 30 minutes later we heard the elevator doors open down the hall and footsteps running toward us. Our surgeon ran into our room with a joyous look on his face. "Mr. and Mrs. Cottrill, the tumor has not grown! In fact, it is shrinking! It is now about the size of a walnut. Do you want me to proceed with the surgery?" Mark and I looked at each other, and with praise to the Lord said, "No! What God has started; He will finish!"

When Matt got back to the room, he was more alert than we had seen him in days. His fever was gone. His eyes were shining. He said, "Mommy, I'm hungry! Can I have a cheeseburger?" Within 48 hours we were dismissed and on our way home with our healthy, happy son.

He has never had a kidney problem since that

long ago day.

Lesson Learned: God is a miracle worker.

He is the one you praise; he is your God who performed for you those great and awesome wonders you saw with your own eyes.
Deuteronomy 10:21 NIV

My Prayer Journey: Lessons Learned

22

It was a beautiful May afternoon in 1984. The grass was at its greenest, the spring flowers were blooming, and the birds were singing. The perfect day to go for a walk. Matt rode behind me on his bike while I pushed baby Nathan in his stroller. We walked our usual route through our neighborhood, keeping our eyes peeled for soda bottles or milk jugs we could redeem for deposits. Some days we could get enough to splurge on an ice cream cone for the boys.

It was a good day and I was enjoying the walk, when I noticed an uneasiness. It was a feeling I recognized. I had felt it before we relocated from St. Paul to Bourbon and from Bourbon to Bucyrus. It was a limbo kind of emotion that comes before change. I pushed it to the recesses of my mind. Surely I was wrong. Mark had said nothing of making any changes. Why would we do that? Our church had grown to about 60, the finances were getting a bit easier, and we were looking at buying another property. Things were finally going our way. I truly loved our church family. Many of them had been converted under our ministry, teaching, and care. They were spiritual offspring. We were bonded with this wonderful church family.

I pushed the feeling aside and refused to verbalize it to anyone. "Let's not make it real," I thought. The feeling seemed to lessen. When it would surface ever so slightly, I would stop it dead in its tracks, refusing to go to the Lord in prayer to explore it. "I love this place, Lord! We came here to see a strong church established and the city of Bucyrus touched by Your truth. Please don't let this be You!"

July came and Mark had scheduled a revival. The evangelist and his wife were friends from our Bible College days. We enjoyed their company, and their ministry was encouraging and stabilizing for our little congregation. One day the evangelist's wife and I were going to the store together, and in casual conversation, I mentioned to her about my feeling that I was afraid something was going to be changing for us. She replied, "Have you talked to Mark about it?" Naturally, that would be what should have happened, but I had to admit, "No, I haven't, I don't want it to be real." Her wise reply hit home. "Not wanting it to be real doesn't make it so. You need to speak to your husband. If it is an accurate unsettling you are perceiving, he will be feeling it, too. If not, then you can sleep easier tonight." Thelma's advice rang true.

Within the next week or two, while we were driving in the car, I took the plunge and asked the

My Prayer Journey: Lessons Learned

question. Please note, I still had not talked to the Lord about it. I was continuing to pray for more souls to be added to the church in Bucyrus, but I would not entertain an audience with God about leaving them behind.

"Mark, do you feel anything in your spirit about our future here?" My inquiry was followed by a long pause, and then, "Why do you ask?" I had to own it then. "I have felt the uneasiness of something changing for us since May, but I didn't want to say anything." Well, Mark's response did not make me sleep easier that night. He, too, was feeling the restlessness of change approaching.

At this point, we did agree to pray about it and leave our hearts and minds open to the leading of God. Neither one of us had anything more concrete than that a change was coming.

The summer slid by with bake sales, BBQs, and fun days of fund raisers filling the calendar as usual. The boys were growing, and it was time to enroll Matt in first grade. We were praying about the future, but neither of us had heard any more specific direction.

September came and went with the leaves changing colors and sweaters coming out of the closets. Fans went to the basement, and chili made its reappearance on the menu. The routine was normal. Then one October Sunday, as we were getting ready to leave for our evening service, the phone rang.

In those days the phone still hung on the wall, with long extension cords that would enable you to move about the room with the phone receiver cradled between your head and shoulder, while continuing to do your work. When I heard the phone ring, I knew Mark had answered. When I walked into the kitchen, I realized he had stretched the cord to the basement with the door shut. "Hmmmm… who could it be?" I wondered.

We were needing to leave for service, and Mark was still talking on the phone. "Must be something serious," I mused. Finally, Mark came upstairs but did not make eye contact with me. I was curious, but decided we did not have time for a lengthy discussion. On the way to the church, he told me it was an important phone call, and we would need to talk about it at length after the service.

I prayed during prayer service and in the altar that evening, asking for direction and wisdom. When we were home and the boys tucked in, the discussion began. The call was from the pastor at the church in Bourbon. Mark had been in prayer that afternoon and was impressed to call that pastor and tell him he was feeling a burden to return. As Mark went to make the call, the phone rang in his hand and it was the pastor. He told Mark, "I am getting ready to resign as pastor here, and I think you are the man to succeed me."

I balked. No! This surely could not be what

My Prayer Journey: Lessons Learned

God wanted! We couldn't leave all our spiritual 'babies' to go back there. We already had spent time there, why would God want us to return? Why?! Why?! Why?!

I cried that night. Lying in the darkness, cradled in each other's arms, Mark whispered, "We have to do this, it's the Lord's will. I feel a confirmation about this."

The next day my stubbornness got the best of me. At breakfast I asked, "Why did you get a confirmation and I didn't? Is this not about my life too?" Mark wisely replied, "We are one, my confirmation is your confirmation." I may have submitted on the outside, but in my heart I was rebellious. The next days were difficult emotionally. I could not submit to the plan. I was in a place that we had given ourselves wholeheartedly. We had carved out a work, and the church was taking shape. There were seemingly a million times over, in the past five years, that we could have packed our bags and left running with our tails between our legs! But now…?!?!

In the weeks that followed, we waited on God. I repeated my complaint in prayer many times to the Lord, "Why can't I get a confirmation?"

In early October, I started feeling sick. I carried a low-grade fever and had pain in my back. Nausea was dominating me and it became a chore to get through the day. Four days later, we agreed I should see a doctor. That began four weeks of pain and suffering with a congenital kidney ailment that was making itself known. I was admitted to the hospital and subjected to some tests and scans, IV antibiotics, and the deep, medicated sleep of morphine. I was experiencing excruciating pain. The medicine would knock me out, and then as it wore off, I would come to in a fog.

One night, as Mark was leaving to go home, we prayed together for my healing. After his departure, I was given my night-time dose of medication and fell into an induced deep sleep. Two hours later, I was suddenly wholly and completely awake. No fog. No pain. Awake and aware that Jesus was in the room. I did not physically see Him, but He was nonetheless there, and I recognized His presence. He spoke to me and said, "I will confirm this to you with an 87% vote." As I laid in that white-sheeted bed, adjusting first the head and then my feet, looking for not only physical comfort but relief from the embarrassment I felt, He left. I felt corrected and ashamed that I had insisted on my own selfish notification from a sovereign God. I did not tell anyone what I had experienced that night.

I was discharged later that week, and the call came from the Bourbon United Pentecostal Church inviting us to come and interview for the newly vacated pastor position. We traveled there in mid-November, preached, fellowshipped, and talked with the deacons. On Tuesday before Thanksgiving

My Prayer Journey: Lessons Learned

the church held an election.

We were sitting in our dining room in Bucyrus when the phone rang. Mark answered, and immediately I knew it was 'the call.' I wrote a note to my husband, "What was the percent of the vote?" He shook his head and wrote, "I don't need to know." I scribbled back, "I need to know." He asked the question and wrote in big numbers: 87%.

It wasn't 85%, or 90%. It was exactly as He said: 87%!

Lesson Learned: God goes before us.

> A man's heart deviseth his way: but the LORD directeth his steps.
>
> Proverbs 16:9 KJV

Notes

My Prayer Journey: Lessons Learned

23

The experiences we had gleaned from the wilderness in Bucyrus were apparently concluding. How could we say good-bye to our beloved church family? Although God had now confirmed His will to me and I felt at peace in my core about our future, there was still the announcement to be made and the good-byes to be said. My heart was full, thinking about the connections we felt with so many of these precious people: Jack and Marilyn Cox and their kids Chris and Tara, the O'Hara's, Steve, the Green's, the Brown's, and others. We also had frequent visits from the White's, a missionary couple. These sweet people had become woven into the fabric of our souls. How could we say farewell? I cried out in anguish to the Lord to send help.

As the time drew near, it was announced that there was a pastoral anniversary banquet being planned in our honor. We were closing out five years as pastor. In celebrating this milestone, we felt torn as we knew that the next week-end we would be announcing our resignation.

And so it was. The date was set and the letter

was written and prepared for the following week-end. I was feeling so lost and filled with dread as Sunday approached. My sister and brother-in-law were sensitive to the Lord and called to offer moral support for our announcement. They were planning to leave as soon as possible after work on Friday and drive the six hours to be there with us for the week-end.

The Sunday evening service concluded with a closing prayer. My pastor husband asked everyone to be seated for a special announcement. I felt the lump in my throat began to form as my sister squeezed my hand. As Mark tearfully read the letter, people began to quietly cry, some staring in disbelief.

I remember feeling so thankful that we had family there to support us in this difficult week-end. When we were dismissed, our church family hugged our necks and kissed our cheeks. Jo Ella and Gary stood nearby to help with the boys and to help us be strong in the face of the emotional closure to this chapter in our lives.

My Prayer Journey: Lessons Learned

Lesson Learned: Moral support is valuable. Note to self, offer it when needed.

"…and they sent Barnabas to Antioch. When he arrived and saw the grace of God [that was bestowed on them], he rejoiced and began to encourage them all with an unwavering heart to stay true and devoted to the Lord.
Acts 11:22-23 AMP

Notes

My Prayer Journey: Lessons Learned

24

Change. Who embraces change? At that time in my life, not me! I loved the familiar and the comfort of routine. After we moved back to Bourbon in January 1985, not only did the demographics change, but my life changed in every way. Contrast pastoring a home missions church of 60 people with a big percentage of them being your own spiritual babies, to a seasoned, 4th generation congregation. Those two experiences are not in the same ball park. Compare living in a town of nearly 13,000 to a small burg of 1600. Restaurants, stores, parks; the choices were reduced greatly. Consider differences between renting a home and becoming first time home owners. I believe buying a home and obtaining a mortgage are in the top ten of the most stressful life experiences. There was one luxury that was a welcomed change—the opportunity for my husband to be a full-time pastor and the ability for me to remain unemployed for the first time in our marriage. Life changed, as it does, for anyone picking up stakes and moving to a different state.

Mark and I were just 29 years old. We had five

years of pastoring under our belts, along with a history with most of the people in Bourbon. We were accustomed to leading in praise and worship, with exuberance and abandon, as the Scriptures direct. Enter into His gates with thanksgiving, and into His courts with praise! Clap your hands all ye people, shout with the voice of triumph! Lift your hands, stand to your feet, and be joyous in His presence! We would come to worship together and see the Lord do marvelous things.

However, the Bourbon church was not accustomed to quite as much spontaneity in worship. Their usual services, though sincere, felt quite 'dry' to our praise-filled tongues. I remember coming home from church, in those early months, with tears in our eyes and hunger for a deeper peace and satisfaction that comes from being in His loving presence when the congregation is in one mind and one accord.

We began to make it a matter of specific prayer. Every day we would beseech the Lord to help us lead the congregation to a deeper level of worship. We fasted and prayed some more. We would go to church determined to worship openly and honestly even if we were the only two.

It was difficult to be the only one standing, eyes closed, hands lifted, worshipping, and moving into His presence. Of course, after getting there, you could soon forget you were alone because in His presence you are not lonely.

My Prayer Journey: Lessons Learned

As the weeks and months passed, our prayers, examples, and hunger for the deep things of God began to inspire others. Thirty-five years later, we enjoy the sweet abandon of worship in a sanctuary that runs deep in worship before the throne of God!

Lesson Learned: Specific prayer reaps specific answers.

> Be careful for nothing; but in everything by prayer and supplication with thanksgiving let your requests be made known unto God.
> Philippians 4:6 KJV

Notes

My Prayer Journey: Lessons Learned

25

This hard lesson I was about to learn started back in Bucyrus in the spring of 1984. I was sitting at the organ, alternating 1, 3, and 5 chords, tapping out the base tempo with my feet for pre-service music, when I looked at the back of the sanctuary and saw Matt, our oldest son, now five years old, motioning for me to help him. At first, I vacillated between leaving the platform and asking one of the sisters to go and assist him. Glancing at my watch, we still had ten minutes before opening prayer and call to worship, so I hurried back to see what he needed. As I assisted him with his restroom needs, I felt a strange aching and burning in my left side. I doubled over in pain, and the urge to urinate was demanding. As Matt stood outside the door and waited for me, the pain and bright red blood was frightening! My husband rushed me to the hospital as our church family began a prayer meeting.

This event began a three-year siege of painful, nausea-filled days for me as a 28-year-old mother of two young boys. Doctor's appointments, hospital stays, tests, IV's, medicines, and did I say… pain…filled my days and nights.

After many weeks it was determined that I was dealing with a rather common congenital malady for girls. This malformation of the ureters allows urine to reflux back into the kidney, causing frequent urinary tract infections. This problem is usually diagnosed and repaired with surgery by the time a child is five or six years old. My condition was just now being discovered after twenty-nine years, and my left kidney was now screaming out the insult of years of asymptomatic infection. I was hospitalized so many times (both in Bucyrus and in Bourbon) for pain and infection over the next three years that we lost count of the occurrences. The procedures and the failed surgeries were mounting up, as were our unpaid bills. I began to feel depressed and useless. My mother would come and stay as long as possible to help with childcare and housework. My mother-in-law did what she could on weekends when she wasn't working her full-time job during the week. I remember being so weary with it all that I asked the Lord to take me if He was not going to heal me. I was pulling my family down being a very expensive invalid.

  I had been seeing a urologist in a nearby city and he was becoming more baffled and less encouraging. Finally, the day came when he admitted, "I have nothing else for you." He then referred me to an apparently well-known urologist in Indianapolis. While we were there, the General

My Prayer Journey: Lessons Learned

Conference for the United Pentecostal Church was convened in St. Louis, Missouri. At a prayer meeting there, an evangelist friend requested prayer for me.

Their prayers were answered with a miracle. When I left that hospital, I walked out pain free and infection free. It has been nearly forty years since that ordeal, and I have had no recurrences or complications since. The Lord himself healed me that day, lying in that Indianapolis hospital room, while the people of God prayed in that St. Louis Convention Center.

It was during this three-year nightmare that I learned compassion. Prior to this experience I had mentally judged people after surgeries and sicknesses. If they did not bounce back and move on rather quickly, I would think, "Come on, quit milking this for all it's worth." I never spoke the words, but the sentiments were, nonetheless, in my heart. I never realized I was uncompassionate, but I was, and this lesson was a hard schoolmaster.

Lesson Learned: Compassion

> Finally, be ye all of one mind, having compassion one of another, love as brethren, be pitiful, be courteous:
>
> 1 Peter 3:8 KJV

Notes

My Prayer Journey: Lessons Learned

26

The windows were steam covered and the air held the smells of Thanksgiving dinner. Turkey, dressing, and dumplings, always on the menu for family dinners, had been prepared, and were roasting, baking, and bubbling. There were tables of baked bread and desserts, all soon to be enjoyed by those who had come to celebrate the holiday with us. Our home was filled with the sounds of laughter and the chatter of several conversations being spoken simultaneously. The kids were playing, the adults visiting, and I was making the umpteenth pot of coffee. It was a happy day. One that I had been anticipating with joy. We were setting up a favorite board game for those wanting to play, as the cooks continued the meal preparation.

Sitting down to take a little break, I heard the familiar voice of God. He brought our good friends, Jack and Marilyn's, faces into my mind. I saw them clearly and felt impressed to call them now. I often prayed that I would be sensitive to the nudges of the Holy Ghost, that I would hear His voice clearly, and be immediately obedient to

His instructions. I excused myself from the room and made my way down the hall to our bedroom, shutting the door behind me. I reached for the bedside phone and punched in their number.

On the second ring, Jack answered the phone. "Happy Thanksgiving," I said. His emotional voice uttered a "Hello" as Jack continued, "You have no idea! You have no idea!" He then went on to further explain, "Marilyn and I were sitting here alone and wondering where God was. I had prayed, God if you are there, please let someone call who will encourage us in You!" Jack continued, "We prayed that, the phone rang, and it was you!"

After a long conversation about the Lord and His goodness and great Love for us, we ended the conversation. I was overjoyed to have been alert in the Holy Ghost and useful to Him, and they had the assurance that God truly was interested in them and was present in their time of need.

Lesson Learned: Respond immediately.

> "Many O LORD my God, are thy wonderful works which thou hast done, And thy thoughts which are to us-ward: They cannot be reckoned up in order unto thee: If I would declare and speak of them, They are more than can be numbered."
>
> Psalm 40:5 KJV

My Prayer Journey: Lessons Learned

27

My heart seemed to lurch up into my throat as I was suddenly awakened. It was a warm summer's night on a small lake in the Upper Peninsula of Michigan. I was sleeping soundly in our little, rustic, vacation cabin, when suddenly I was propelled from my bed; literally, drawn up from bed onto my feet, fully awake.

It only took a split second for me to realize that the Spirit had awakened me. As He drew me up out of the bed, I went to the living room area and knelt at an old couch on the worn carpet of the living room floor. I knew that I had been called to an urgent midnight prayer meeting. As I began to travail, it was but moments until I knew the subject of this call to prayer: a co-worker and friend. And the urgency was unmistakable. The prayer time lasted into the wee hours of the morning, when exhausted, I felt the burden melt away. I dropped back into bed with the assurance that the battle was won.

When morning broke, breakfast finished, and my three guys were out the door to fish on the lake, I sat at the table and wrote my friend a long letter about what had happened the night before. I mailed it with a prayer that he would one day be delivered from his suffering.

A few days later I ran into my friend and asked if he had received my letter. With tears in his eyes, he confided in me that the night I was praying, he was contemplating suicide. This man still lives today and gives thanks for God's call to prayer on his behalf.

I will never forget that long-ago night that was transformed into a spiritual battle zone. I am forever grateful for that call to prayer during the silence of the night.

Lesson Learned: Some prayers are timely and urgent. I should listen and respond when He calls.

> "And I heard a voice from heaven, as the voice of many waters, and as the voice of great thunder…"
>
> Revelation 14:2 KJV

> I call on you, my God, for you will answer me; turn your ear to me and hear my prayer.
>
> Psalm 17:6 MSG

My Prayer Journey: Lessons Learned

28

Pitiful. That's the word. The Lord told me I was pitiful, and He was right.

The boys were growing up. We had gotten through elementary school with few hurdles. They both had good grades, played hard, and our home was filled with laughter. Those years were filled with church, ball games, church, picnics, church, and yearly family vacations. We were thrilled, when at the age of eight, Matt returned home from his first church camp filled with the Holy Ghost. He had received it during a morning service, worshipping at his pew. The camp evangelist's wife had been praying with Matt, and she reported to us his sweet experience. His dad baptized him in Jesus' name that weekend. We were so happy to witness our son Nathan's infilling and water baptism in our own church altars when he was five. I was standing near and heard him speak in other tongues as the Spirit gave him the utterance and watched as his little face glowed with the light of God's love. The joy of seeing your children receive this beautiful gift is unmatched for a parent.

Matthew had always been a bright and

energetic boy. In my own mind, he well represented the character of Tigger in Winnie the Pooh. He bounced here and there with an enthusiasm for life, and always embraced the spirit of 'the more the merrier.'

As he matured into a teenager, his inborn, strong will became a daily challenge. He not only pushed the envelope, he knocked down doors to get his way. As he neared graduation, his spiritual hunger lagging, he was not sure of the pathway for his future. He talked about joining the military, looked at technical schools, and employment. Very late, Matt applied to Indiana Bible College and left in the fall of 1996 to attend.

His heart was not really in it, and as he ran with others immature in their walks with God, he spiraled downward. His independence from us and the home church did not serve him well.

He came back home after three semesters, completely backslidden. He moved back into our home, but was not amiable to house rules. Over the course of the next two years, we were heavily burdened for his soul.

I began to fast and pray. Looking back on it, I felt quite sorry for myself. His actions were embarrassing us in front of our church, our friends, and our colleagues. But more than any of that, the weight of his soul on my heart was more than I could bear, and yet bear it I did, day after day, night after night.

My Prayer Journey: Lessons Learned

One day as I was sitting in the recliner in our living room, I cried out in prayer until I could not cry anymore. My energy was spent, when suddenly I felt that familiar presence speak clearly to me. He said, "You are pitiful." I replied, "I know I am pitiful, Lord, and I need You to help me." His reply was, "Give him to Me." I sniffled into another wadded-up tissue and said, "Yes, Lord, that is what I will do."

And I tried to do just that, I really did. But when I got up from the chair to make supper, the deep heavy sigh was still there, and the lump in my throat was still frozen in place.

A few weeks later, things had gotten worse. Matt was regularly missing church services. He was out late at night and refused to communicate with us about his plans or his whereabouts. The front row seat to his lifestyle choices was a nightmare. One night, travailing at my bedside for him to come home, Matt returned. He walked past our bedroom and slammed his door shut. At least we knew where he was.

I kept saying, "I give him to You, Lord, I give him to You." But my emotions did not change, and I was far from having peace about his future. The thought of your own child spending eternity in hell's flames is the worst burden a God-fearing mother can bear. It was the most miserable time of my existence. Sickness, poverty, and the loneliness were cake walks compared to those trying days.

I decided to fast and pray that God would show me how to give Matthew to Him. It was on the fifth day of a seven day fast, early in the morning, lying face down on the altar at the church, organ side, that I found that place. I remember the tear-soaked, blue, tweed carpet beneath my face and the coolness of the room. I can still remember when Jesus approached me and said, "Ok, now give Matt to me. You are not, nor can you be, his savior." Then, in that moment, I felt the knots in my stomach dissolve, the lump in my throat disappear, and the weight—that awful weight of Matt's soul—was lifted from me.

My prayer time finished, my goal achieved, I went back home to bed to sleep more deeply than I had slept in weeks.

Later that day as I did the dishes, I was singing and at peace when Matt came home, walked through the kitchen, and went to take a shower. As was his normal conduct, he would have left afterwards without saying a word. But as he made his way through the kitchen, I turned from the sink, wiping my hands with a dish towel. "Matt, I need to tell you something." Rolling his eyes, he replied, "Do we have to do this again?" I informed him that I had given him to the Lord, that I was no longer going to stand in God's way, and that He would be his parent now. I saw a hint of fear in his eyes, but without pause, Matt responded, "Are you done yet?" I replied, "As a matter of fact, I am!" He left without another word, but that was the day that Matt started his journey in a new direction.

Was the result instantaneous? No, but over the next eighteen months, God led Matt back full circle. And as for me, I enjoyed the calm assurance that all would be well with his soul.

Lesson Learned: I am not the Savior.

> I, even I, am the LORD, and apart from me there is no savior.
> Isaiah 43:11 NIV

Notes

My Prayer Journey: Lessons Learned

29

We were making plans to attend the United Pentecostal Church General Conference in North Carolina in 2008. Matt and his wife Brandie were making plans as well. Their three children were going to stay with a loving family in their church where they pastored in Michigan City, Indiana (Matt really did come full circle!). We were excited about being with our kids and were anticipating the conference. The day came when they left their home to make the long drive to the conference. As they were packing the kids, Carter, then six, complained of a sore throat. Feeling his forehead, he felt warm to his mother's touch and at the last minute, the decision was made for Carter to come with his parents.

They arrived in North Carolina a few hours before the Thursday evening service was to begin. Mark and I offered to stay in the hotel with Carter and let them attend the service. Carter came into the room feverish and lethargic. I sat him on my lap, gently rocking him and whispering a prayer. He had not wanted anything to eat all that day. As the evening unfolded, Carter became more active and he slid off my lap to play with his cars and army men on the floor with Paw-Paw. Before the hour had passed, he asked for something to eat. Calling room service, we ordered his favorites—a cheeseburger and fries. When his parents returned, they were thrilled to see him so animated and happy.

 Two days later, the Children's Ministries were holding a service in a conference arena room. As I was leaving my Ladies' Ministries meeting, a text came in from Brandie. Carter was in the altar seeking the Holy Ghost. I ran through the venue towards the room. As I found it, I entered the large altar area full of praying children. I saw his little blonde head and made a bee-line to the front. As I excused my way to the corner of the platform, I made eye contact with the evangelist who was praying with him. We were acquaintances. She mouthed the words, pointing to Carter, "Is he yours?" I replied with the nodding of my head. She motioned me closer, and just as I nudged my way over in front of him, he turned his face upward and began speaking in other tongues as the Spirit gave him the utterance. He was experiencing the Acts 2:38 message for himself! The joy of the Lord shown from his little face and I was overjoyed to be a witness to his new birth.

 I felt as if the Lord had given me a very special gift that day as well as my sweet Carter!

My Prayer Journey: Lessons Learned

Lesson Learned: His blessings are abundant and He bestows them freely. Even though I never verbally asked the Lord for me to be able to see my grandchildren filled with the Holy Ghost, He knew the desire of my heart.

> And his mercy is on them that fear him from generation to generation.
> Luke 1:50 KJV

Notes

My Prayer Journey: Lessons Learned

30 Phyllis was small in stature, but her quiet voice of wisdom was large. I admired this dark-haired, plain woman. She was always quietly present at church in Bourbon. She taught Sunday School, cleaned the church, and sat on the front row. She became an elementary school teacher as an older, non-traditional student. She raised four foster children after her own five kids. She was a force to be reckoned with. One day she was in the church basement as I came down the concrete steps. I was round with the weight of my first pregnancy. She questioned, "Have you been praying for your baby?" I was a young and inexperienced 23-year-old girl. My face registered a blank, non-verbal response. She proceeded, "You're starting late. Pray for your baby, for his/her life, his/her spouse."

Her advice was valuable, and I took it seriously from that moment on. So, when I was expecting my second child, Nathan, I did not start late. I prayed for his spouse, whoever and wherever she may be. As Nate entered his adult life and began his career in social services, he asked me one day, "Mom, would you be disappointed if

I never married?" I replied, "Of course not. That is a decision that only you can make. My only regret would be that you would grow old alone." I recalled my many prayers for his helpmeet and prayed, "Lord, Your will be done."

Nate was 28 and had not yet had a long-term, meaningful relationship. He was experiencing burn-out in his demanding career. The government cutbacks were closing his office in Bloomington, Indiana. He made the decision to move back to Bourbon and seek employment there.

Soon after his return, I saw him in the parking lot as I was exiting the church. He was standing next to a yellow Volkswagen and its owner, Kayla. I heard his laughter and saw Kayla's smiling face upturned to his. My heart skipped a beat.

Kayla had been raised in our church. She had always been a special girl. Her walk with God was committed. She was self-sufficient and earning her degree in nursing. She was beautiful. She was perfect.

And the rest of the story… she became the daughter-in-law of my prayers! Thank you, Phyllis. Thank You, God. This union has given me my two beautiful and loving grand-daughters, Adeline Jane, and Blair Elizabeth. Even though at this writing they are ages seven and four, I am praying for their spouses.

It is of note, that though I started praying late for Matthew's spouse, the Lord blessed Mark and me with Matt's wife, Brandie. She, too, is an absolute answer to prayer. She is beautiful. She is perfect.

Lesson Learned: You can never start too early in praying for your children's future.

> I will sing of the mercies of the LORD forever: With my mouth will I make known thy faithfulness to all generations.
>
> Psalm 89:1 KJV

Notes

My Prayer Journey: Lessons Learned

31

Satan is such a name-calling, low down, conniving liar. That day he called me an ugly horse!

It was literally the turn of the century. Matt would be married, and Nathan would leave for Indiana University in the fall of 2000. Matt had allowed the Lord to turn his life around. He had learned the hard way, from many mistakes. He was going to take steps toward the calling God had on his life. Nathan was never one to openly defy us, the compliant, second-born. But as he was spreading his wings, he took a path that would cause us much concern and sleepless nights.

As many other eighteen-year-olds, he would make some immature and expensive mistakes in his new-found collegiate freedom. Church attendance became a back-place priority. Following that, his prayer life became non-existent. No one can spiritually survive these circumstances for long.

I had learned my lesson about taking on the weight of his soul but prayed daily for him to have wisdom, and to learn quickly what was important. We were disturbed and disappointed, when during four years of college, there would be jail time, court appearances, and alcohol miseries.

One morning, as I prepared for work, I was getting dressed and felt impressed to wear my long, uncut hair down. As a nurse, hair hanging down past your waist is not a professional style. But I obeyed the notion and went to the church to pray.

Later that day, Nate was to appear before a judge for a DUI offense. The mother in me wanted to be by his side, but I remembered the lesson of giving Matt to the Lord to parent and followed suit this time. Lying on my face behind the back pew in the sanctuary at the church, I wept into my hair as I asked God to dispatch angels to accompany Nate into the court room. I pled with God to do whatever He needed to do so that Nathan would learn the most out of this lesson. It was a fervent, intercessory, heart-felt prayer experience I will never forget. Indeed, every time I walk in that area of the back of our church, it flashes before me. I have not laid memorial stones there in remembrance, but remember I do. Leaving late for work, there was no time to run home to put my hair up in my typical style.

I arrived at work that morning very conscious of my hair. My co-workers had never seen it down. It was strait, thankfully clean, and just pulled back to the nape of my neck, hanging down my back. The enemy started to berate me and call me "ugly."

My Prayer Journey: Lessons Learned

Satan continued, "Your hair definitely looks like a pony tail. Yes! That's it! A horse's tail—that is what you are. Silly to think that leaving your hair down would make prayers any more valuable or effective." Still, I knew what God's Word declares about a woman's uncut hair having power with the angels.

Trying to focus on the tasks at hand, I prepared for what would be, as always, a very demanding and busy clinic day. Before the first patient arrived, a co-worker from the check-out desk wandered past my cubicle. With my back to her, I heard her exclaim, "Jane, your hair!" With the lying words of Satan still in my mind, I repeated, "I know, I didn't have time this morning to put it up! It looks like a horse's tail." She replied, "No! Not at all! You look…you look…angelic!" She used the word angelic! As she went on her way, a tear trickled down my cheek in thanksgiving that I had heard and responded to the Lord's instructions.

As the demands of the day presented themselves, I had little time to concentrate on what might be happening in the courtroom four hours away. When I did have a break, I placed a call to Nathan. We had not spoken and he did not know anything about my prayer petitions.

He reported that it was very crowded when he went to the room to await being called before the judge. He remarked that his thoughts were, "What am I doing here? This is not who I am." He sat down with an empty chair on either side of him. Strangely, as the room filled up, no one sat in those chairs, even though some sat on the floor. As his turn was called, he stood up and reportedly felt as if he had someone on either side of him. He said he approached the bench, spoke with the judge, and never felt as if he were alone. "I had total confidence."

When I told Nathan that he had been accompanied by angels that day, he did not disagree.

Lesson Learned: My submission to His word is powerful

> For this cause ought the woman to have power on her head because of angels.
> I Corinthians 11:10 KJV

My Prayer Journey: Lessons Learned

32

The eastern sky was turning pink when I pulled into the church parking lot. As I exited the car, I saw a young man sitting alone with his back against the neighbor's garage. I wondered if he was sleeping. At that time, he lifted his sleepy eyes and responded as I said, "Good morning." I had never seen him before, but this mother of boys always has a soft spot in her heart for the 'fellows.' I asked him if he was okay, to which he replied, "A little sore and a lot hungry." I told him to wait and I would be back.

I went to the mini-mart a block away and grabbed a large sweet and creamy coffee, two donuts, and a steaming ham and cheese croissant. Arriving back at the church, the young man had stretched and smoothed his unruly hair into a less bedraggled style. As I opened my window and handed him the breakfast, his eyes looked into mine and he whispered, "Thank you, ma'am." I told him that I would be praying for him and that Jesus loved him. He thanked me again, and as he turned to walk down the alley, he stopped again and said, "I think Jesus sent you for me today, and

I thank you again."

It was in those early Bourbon pastorate days that I began to be drawn to pray early in the morning, before getting the day started. I would be awakened with people on my mind and heart, and I could not do anything but pray. I would get up early on dark winter mornings, or spring and summer dawns, and dress in silence to walk or drive to the church. I have spent many an hour, through these many years, at the altar all by myself. The habit soon became a lifestyle, and the communion I found with the Lord during those times sustained me.

I have gained wisdom, fought spiritual battles, lavished praise on the Lord, and been in awe of His presence in these wonderful seasons of prayer. At times, down through the years, others have joined me there in the stillness of the morning to approach the throne of God. There have been times, with the collective church, that we have held 6 AM prayer meetings. I have found, whether alone or in a group, early morning is the best time to seek God and get His direction and answers. There are Scriptures that direct us to pray in the morning, even before dawn. Jesus, David, and others prayed during those hours.

One reason there is such a blessing to be had in the morning hours is that you are prioritizing your schedule and putting Him first in your day. It is also helpful to start your day with Him so that

He has the opportunity to direct your path. How can He direct your day if you wait until nightfall to acknowledge Him? Thirdly, starting your day with Him before everyone else is awake and placing their demands on you, your time alone with Him is distraction free!

My prayer times were spent in asking for revival in our congregation, for the salvation of souls in our town, and for our family to be used in ministry.

Lesson Learned: Prioritize prayer early every day.

> My voice shalt thou hear in the morning, O LORD; in the morning will I direct my prayer unto thee, and will look up.
>
> Psalm 5:3 KJV

Notes

My Prayer Journey: Lessons Learned

33

It was May, time for Mother-Daughter banquets and parties. It was 1990, and we were still using the original basement of the oldest part of our building for such events. The room was set and decorated. I had invited my friend, Cammy, to speak, and it was promising to be a good evening. The ladies came in smiling and happy to be together. The food looked good, and dinner was the first order of business. The buffet line formed, and the clink of serving spoons was mixed with chatting and laughter.

With dinner finished, some games played, and announcements for our group done, I introduced Cammy. She began by greeting all these ladies as her friends and family. She had been born in our church when her grand-father pastored there. She was at home. Cammy read her Scripture and began sharing her heart. At some point in her lesson, she was interrupted by metal chairs scooting on the concrete floor and anxious gasps. An elderly lady, Hilda, slid from her chair and onto the floor. Joan, her daughter, knelt beside her. I instructed someone to run upstairs to phone the EMS and to inform the pastor who was in his office. I knelt beside her, asking the Lord not to take her. I felt such a need for the continued, faithful, spiritual support of this long-time saint of God.

Feeling along her neck, I could find no pulse. Looking and listening for breath, I could see no respiration. Hilda was in her late eighties. She had lived a good life, and Joan instructed us not to be heroic. The ladies were praying. My pastor-husband came into the room. He knelt beside Hilda and began to pray. Suddenly, she gasped in a breath of air and opened her eyes. She was weak but responding. Several minutes had passed before the EMT's arrived to check her condition. Pulse and respirations were normal. They did transport her to the hospital, although Hilda insisted that it was not necessary. She was released a day later.

I was thrilled to witness God's hand bringing Hilda back to life. She lived another ten plus years.

Lesson Learned: Jesus does raise the dead to life.

> Wherefore he saith, Awake thou that sleepest, and arise from the dead, and Christ shall give thee light.
>
> Ephesians 5:14 KJV

My Prayer Journey: Lessons Learned

34 In 1999, Matt moved to Florida. If he had done that before I learned that I was not the Savior, I would have had a complete meltdown. But now, having been relieved of the burden of his soul, we helped him pack and waved good-bye, trusting the Lord.

I was on the Indiana District Ladies Committee as Section One Director. It was time for the annual Ladies Conference at Calvary Tabernacle in Indianapolis. In those days, I arrived about two hours before the opening service and prepared to check off my list of duties. I had a taupe-colored, vinyl Day-Timer that kept this impromptu sanguine on course. On the front of that journal was a picture frame that encased a photo of my two beloved sons.

That night's service, though I can't honestly tell you who the speaker was, nor of the message content, I can tell you that the Lord was there in a powerful way. The moving of His Spirit was ministering to our hearts on an individual basis. Digressing, isn't it wonderful that God the Creator, the Savior of the World, can be everything each of us needs at any given moment? The crowd of 2,000 women were, I feel, all being ministered to in their own state of circumstances. Whether sick or distressed, facing financial hardship or divorce, looking for direction or mourning loss, the warm blanket of comfort fluttered down over that conference. I know He met me there that night on my knees.

As I fell on my face, prostrate before the Lord, I held that picture and travailed for my sons, asking God to fulfill His plan in their lives. This was different than any prayer I had prayed before. The intensity was all consuming. It was at least an hour of intercession, tears, and requests to the throne of God. I remember the exhaustion once I was released from the yoke of that prayer meeting. I was as limp as a rag.

A highly respected mentor of mine, Sister Micki Mooney, came to me that night and wept with me as I held that picture to my chest. She joined me in that agony of prayer.

I look back now and know, beyond the shadow of any doubt, He heard and answered our prayers.

My Prayer Journey: Lessons Learned

Lesson Learned: God-called intercession reaps results.

> Likewise, the Spirit helps us in our weakness, for we do not know what to pray for as we ought, but the Spirit himself intercedes for us with groanings too deep for words.
>
> Romans 8:26 ESV

Notes

My Prayer Journey: Lessons Learned

35

We were living busy, indeed, sometimes hectic lives—pastoring, parenting, and providing. Our congregation was growing, and we were in the throes of a building program at the church. I was working full time as an RN; Mark was overseeing the work site and the needs of the congregation. Did I say hectic?

For years, we had been friends with a family that originated in the Bourbon church and had followed their call to pursue full time evangelism and finally an overseas missionary calling. Their children and our two boys grew up together. We fellowshipped as often as possible, enjoying one another's company. We celebrated holidays together, and Mark and I traveled to Europe twice to visit. It was the dearest of friendships. As our kids were growing up and leaving for college and careers, their girls moved back to the states and took up residence in Bourbon. I committed to my friend that I would be their 'mother' on this side of the world. We saw them at church and regularly took them out for meals, or they would come to the house, always welcomed.

Around this time, the relationship started to deteriorate. I honestly do not know what happened. It seemed that suddenly our encouragement and guidance were no longer valued, welcomed, or needed. My heart shattered and my very life seemed to be sucked out of me as I was left alone—so very alone.

The ache in our hearts was real as they made their exit from our lives. Shock and hurt from being suddenly spurned caused a constant ache both day and night in the weeks that followed.

The loss drove me to my knees with no words, just gut-wrenching disbelief, void, and silence. As I regained my voice, I cried to the Lord, "Why?!" The pain was real, the loneliness palpable. Then quietly, tenderly, the Lord surrounded me with His loving arms. He whispered His love to me and said, "And now you know me in the fellowship of My suffering." I did not understand. The fellowship of His suffering had always been the horrible crucifixion, the cross. He explained, "All of My friends forsook Me too. On that night when I needed my companions, I had to stand alone." Then, gently, He told me, "I am a jealous God and want to be your best friend. In the past, you have shared your heart with your friend. I have removed her so that you will find that camaraderie in Me."

That was a hard lesson learned, and although it was a hard pill to swallow, I did become best friends with Jesus. For years He has been my

My Prayer Journey: Lessons Learned

go-to for heart wounds, concerns, worries, and sadness. He has never failed to be that Friend to me.

Years later that friendship was renewed as if nothing ever happened, and we now enjoy time with our friends again.

Lesson Learned: He is a jealous God and wants to be first in our lives.

> That I may know him, and the power of his resurrection, and the fellowship of his sufferings…
>
> Philippians 3:10a KJV

Notes

My Prayer Journey: Lessons Learned

36

It was a gray, chilly day in November, 2005, when our second-born grandson was a scheduled C-section. He would be delivered around 8 AM, and we were excited to welcome another Cottrill into our growing family. As Mark and I arrived at the hospital and made our way to the obstetrics department, we repeated our prayers for all to go well. A few minutes later we caught the first glimpse of our now beloved Dylan through the glass of the nursery. My nursing career has had very little exposure to the labor and delivery experience except during my clinicals. However, I knew immediately that his APGAR scores were mediocre. The blue tint of his lips and the furrowed brow of the nurse as she cleaned him up confirmed my concerns. We made our way into the room as Brandie and Matt were being moved in from delivery. I hugged them and rejoiced and then made my way back to the nursery window. The nurse was conversing with the doctor and Dylan's color had not improved. In fact, now the blue tint was covering his face and his hands looked deeper blue than before. "Oh, Jesus, help!"

We returned to Brandie's bedside as the nurse entered, carrying Dylan all wrapped in the hospital print, blue blanket, his dark-haired head covered in the infant toboggan we have all seen in so many hospital nurseries. The nurse placed Dylan into his mother's arms, allowing those first precious moments to be shared and then proceeded to inform them that Dylan was not doing as well as they would like to see. "He's having difficulty breathing." The alarm registered swiftly on Matt and Brandie's faces as the plan was shared to transport their newborn to the NICU in South Bend.

That same morning, our church was laying to rest a precious saint of God. Her visitation and funeral would be held with Mark officiating. I drove to Bourbon. During that twelve-mile trip, my concern turned to worry, and finally, outright panic took over. Arriving at the church, I filed past the casket, told Mark I could not stay, and headed for South Bend. I called my parents, sisters, and praying friends for their support. Wiping tears away to clear my vision to drive safely, I called out to the Lord. I would find out later that they lost Dylan twice on the ambulance ride from the hospital to South Bend.

As I made my way to the NICU and identified myself as Dylan's grandmother, I was shown to the family waiting room to wait, as the baby was evaluated, hooked up to monitors, and placed in

My Prayer Journey: Lessons Learned

the incubator. After what seemed like hours—in reality about 45 minutes—the pediatrician came and gave me a report. Dylan had been born too early. The OB/GYN had miscalculated his due date. He had been taken by C-section at approximately eight months. His lungs lacked the all-important surfactant that finishes the maturation of the lungs and prepares the baby to breathe. The fact that he weighed six pounds four ounces was helpful in the fight for his life. The doctor said, "Let's cross our fingers and hope." I replied, "I will fold my hands in prayer and hope."

I was allowed to go in for ten minutes every hour. The first time going in my heart pounded in cadence with the beeps and hums of the life-saving machines in the room. I approached the incubator and reached my finger in to stroke his little wrist wrapped in an oxygen monitor. His little feet kicked when I touched him. I told him I was his Maw-Maw and I wasn't leaving. I also told him his mom would come when she could and that Jesus was with him too. My ten minutes ended as I gulped back a lump in my throat and retreated to the little waiting room. I slept on a love seat that night in between hourly visits. The nurses encouraged me to go home and come back in the morning, but I would have none of it.

Several days and nights passed. Brandie and Matt would be able to come to Memorial Hospital soon. It was a Sunday evening. Church was convened in Bourbon, and I knew the congregation was praying. As I sat next to Dylan's incubator, I saw a change come over him. His complexion was pink! He was breathing on his own, according to what I was seeing, and I felt the overshadowing of the Holy Ghost. He was being touched this very moment by my prayer-answering God. He was going to live!

Now, as I type this, Dylan is almost seventeen years old. He is acknowledging a call to ministry and is actively seeking God's direction in his life.

Lesson Learned: Jesus' plan will be worked, as we release it to Him. We must trust Him.

> The Spirit of God hath made me, and the breath of the Almighty hath given me life.
>
> Job 12:16 KJV

My Prayer Journey: Lessons Learned

37

Raising two sons always gave me a soft spot in my heart for the boys of our church. If one was going through a rough time with home, school, his health, or any kind of trouble, this mama's heart felt his pain and was crying out for him in my prayer closet. I would often reach out in situations of adversity to try to assist and be 'on their team' if I could.

There was a waitress at the local diner that Mark and I had befriended, the mother of four sons and two daughters. We did not know it when we met her, but she was a backslidden Pentecostal. Many mornings as she poured our coffee and took our breakfast orders, we would smile and laugh with her, and Mark always invited her to church. After several months, she finally came and brought her family. She prayed through to a renewal in the Holy Ghost and became a faithful member of the church. Her third oldest son, Tom, was in his early teens. He was a kind, hard-working boy, following in his mother's footsteps working in foodservice, first bussing tables and eventually cooking. He also was baptized in water for the remission of his sins and was filled with the Spirit at a young age.

As Tom was growing up, he became involved with drugs and became addicted to nicotine, alcohol, and narcotics. He was not too old when he was first jailed for activities connected with this lifestyle. He put my name on his visitation list, and I would go as often as possible to visit with him through the scratched glass that separated us. I would pray with him as we held our palms to the Plexiglas when our visit concluded. He was always respectful and repentant but could not free himself from the addiction. So, when he would be released, the cycle would start over, and again we would find ourselves visiting in the dingy jail cubicles. Eventually his repeated convictions brought a prison sentence, and my visitations were few and far between as the prison was not in my county. I would write letters and prayed often and fervently for Tom's deliverance from his addiction and for release from prison. Through all of this, I carried Tom close in my heart.

When Tom was nearing his release, my husband and I were invited to speak at a church in Urbana, Illinois. During this visit, the pastor's wife, Brenda, introduced me to her current project. She was working with her husband and church to found a residential recovery center for men with substance abuse. She was passionate, excited, and had done her homework. She, like me, had a heart for young boys in her congregation and

My Prayer Journey: Lessons Learned

had watched as a Sunday School boy had ruined his life with drugs. She states now, "It is one of the most rewarding purposes I have found in life: to see God transform someone from what many consider 'a lost cause' to a person on fire for God, delivered, and ready to give back." In 2006, they opened the doors to Lifeline-Connect, and their endeavor became extremely rewarding. That weekend was spent listening to her dream, touring the yet unfinished dormitory, and watching as she interacted with soon to be staff members of this endeavor. Little did I know that visit was a part of God's plan.

A few months later, Tom was released. I shared with Tom's mom about this facility I had seen and asked her to communicate the possibility of Tom going there to get a fresh start. She was not open to the idea, believing Tom was reformed, had paid his dues, and had learned from his mistakes. I hoped with my heart that she was right. Diane, Tom's mother, had missed him desperately during his incarceration and wanted him home, believing he would come and be faithful to church and stay clean. Tom came to church a couple of times upon his release but soon got a job at a McDonald's that required Sunday work.

I went to McDonald's a few times and would sit with him on his break and watch for signs that things were not well. It was not long before it became evident that his addiction was ruling his life once again.

One Saturday night, I was in travail for Tom's soul, when I felt to call him and tell him about Lifeline-Connect. It would not be easy, but the life he was living was tortuous. He listened. Later that evening, he called and said, "I want to go." While he was of the mindset to take that giant step, my husband quickly made the arrangements with Lifeline-Connect and took Tom, driving late into the night to get him the help he needed.

That has been nearly twenty years ago. My hopes and prayers were answered. Tom is now married, with two sweet children. He is a manager at a nation-wide sandwich restaurant franchise and has recently been appointed as the Sunday School Director for his local church.

Lesson Learned: There are no lost causes.

> Now unto him that is able to do exceeding abundantly above all that we ask or think, according to the power that worketh in us,
> Ephesians 3:20 KJV

My Prayer Journey: Lessons Learned

38

It's a girl! A sweet and welcomed declaration after three generations of Cottrill boys. Morgan Emilee was named by her parents. She was born on May 18th, the same day as her paternal great-grandmother. If she had still been alive, she would have been dancing with glee to know that a girl in the family had been named after her (Adeline Emily). Emilee was spelled differently to include being named for her own mama, Brandie Lee.

She was adorable and it was fun to be buying dresses and dolls. Her pixie-like face and strawberry-blonde hair were perfect. Thank you, Lord, for this precious gift!

Matt and Brandie had been working in our church on the youth team for several years, and the Lord was calling them to pastoring. And so it was, when my little Morgan was only six-months old, the plans were made and the moving van was backed into their driveway. Matt had accepted the invitation to pastor the United Pentecostal Church congregation in Michigan City, Indiana, a little over an hour from Bourbon.

My heart seemed to crack that day sitting on the couch in their small living room as I bounced Morgan on my knees, singing to her, drinking in her sweet face. An hour. That's not so bad, you say. But it seemed bad to this Maw-Maw who had enjoyed her three grandchildren living only blocks away. I had been blessed to hold them in my lap at church, watch them bouncing to the worship music, raising their little hands to copy me, and clapping off beat. Now, that would not be the case.

Though heartsick, I knew with assurance that Matt, Brandie, and the children were moving forward under His direction. So, with my little sweetheart in my arms, I held her close and prayed a prayer of protection and blessing for her young life.

The move happened and we went as often as possible for visits. However, at the time, I was still working as an RN, we were still pastoring full-time, I was leading the Indiana District Ladies Ministries, and our days were full. To further complicate it, Michigan City was in another time zone. So, coming home took "two hours." Our visits were more infrequent than we wanted.

Mark and I had gone to a cabin in the woods of Pigeon Forge owned by our dear friends. It was a refreshing haven of rest that we ran to on occasion when life was closing in. I was sitting at the counter in the kitchen working a jigsaw puzzle when I saw a text video come in from Brandie.

My Prayer Journey: Lessons Learned

As I picked it up, the video was of then five-year-old Morgan. She was at the altar in a Michigan City church prayer meeting. Her little eyes were squeezed shut, and her cheeks were wet with tears of joy as she was being filled with the Spirit of God. Her little voice was uttering words in another language.

I was thrilled and wept as we watched the video over and over. Even though I wasn't holding Morgan on my lap in church services anymore, He had blessed us with getting to "witness" her beautiful infilling.

Morgan is currently fourteen and loves the Lord, lives for Him, and embraces His Word.

Lesson Learned: He is able and willing to give us the desires of our heart.

> Delight thyself also in the LORD; And he shall give thee the desires of thine heart.
> Psalm 37:4 KJV

Notes

My Prayer Journey: Lessons Learned

39

It was a cold and snowy, dark night in 2010. We had finished having an early family Christmas celebration as my daughter-in-law, Brandie, corralled our three grandchildren into her vehicle. She was leaving for Florida to be with her family for the holidays. I understood her desire and need to go, but the weather report was not good, and my mother's heart was already worrying about her making the trip alone with my sweet grandbabies. Matt was working nights on the Michigan City, Indiana, police force. He did not have any vacation time to join her.

I finished cleaning up the mountain of ribbons and wrapping paper, moved into the kitchen to tidy up, and make the left overs into a buffet that we could visit as the evening wore on. A couple of hours passed. The snowfall was dumping inches on the ground outside my dark windows. The radar revealed the dark blue of heavy snow over the entire region. My mind was on the kids. "How was Brandie and my precious grands?" I wondered and whispered prayers.

Matt was in a recliner in the living room when

his cell phone rang. Brandie was near Rantoul, Illinois, and had gotten off at the exit as the white outs had blinded her into disorientation. She was hoping to get off the highway and wait out the storm but found herself in a slide off on a country road. Her gas tank was low, and her cell phone power less full than her gas tank. Matt and Mark discussed worried options of responding.

I went down the hall to my bedroom, falling on my face by the bed. I cried out with a loud voice to our God. I begged and interceded for angelic assistance for my most precious kids. The prayers continued into the evening.

Brandie, too, was becoming adept in prayer. I am convinced that our prayers mingled together rising into the throne room. As the temperatures dropped and the blinding blizzard continued, there came a knock at Brandie's driver's side window. There stood a man asking her if he could be of assistance. He was driving a red pick-up truck, with a plow on the front, and had a tow rope. He proceeded to pull her out of the ditch. He informed her he was from the area and cleared the road and made a way for her to get to the nearby gas station.

In the meantime, Matt had contacted the pastor of the nearby United Pentecostal Church congregation. These precious people, the Kings, met them at the station and led them back to their church where warm bedrooms and provisions awaited them.

My Prayer Journey: Lessons Learned

My grandchildren remember this as an adventure and do not recall any anxiety or fear with the recollection.

Lesson Learned: Angels are real and respond to orders from the Lord.

The angel of the LORD encampeth round about them that fear him, and delivereth them.
Psalm 34:7 KJV

Notes

My Prayer Journey: Lessons Learned

40 Life was speeding around on a merry-go-round that made falling into the bed for a few short hours a relief but certainly not a refreshing. I was running on fumes: teaching Sunday School, leading our prayer meetings, directing the choir, becoming a grandmother, and working as an RN forty hours a week. While this was wearing me out, I was elected as the Ladies Ministries President for the Indiana District United Pentecostal Church. The day I learned that news, I was having lunch with Nathan in a downtown diner in Bloomington, Indiana. Matt called me from the conference floor and told me, while Mark was accepting the position for me! I felt like I would be sick to my stomach. I argued with Matt that surely this was a cruel joke. He assured me it was not. How was I going to add another ball to my juggling routine?!

I was overwhelmed. I was anxious. I was astonished. I could not imagine what this new position would do to me physically, mentally, or spiritually. During this time, when we would be retiring for the day, I would tell Mark, "Something has to give. I'm either going to have a heart attack or a stroke. I can't keep doing this."

I was providing our health insurance through my employer and felt responsible for this, so I thought reducing my hours was not an option. I had promised God when I went back to school to work on my nursing degree that I would not let it affect my involvement in my ministries for the church, so I couldn't find relief there. I spoke with Brother Stroup, Indiana District Superintendent, that night at the conference and told him I did not feel qualified or able to accept the position for which I had been elected. He informed me the election was final. He encouraged me to accept it and let the Lord lead me and help me in the endeavor.

And so, the merry-go-round sped up.

One Sunday afternoon, while Mark was in Burma, ministering at a conference, I experienced an explosion in the back of my head that threw me to our living room floor. I really don't know if I became unconscious, or if I did, how long I laid on the floor. I do remember crawling to our kitchen, reaching up onto the counter for my cell phone, and looking at it as I thought, 'I should call someone.' Unfortunately, I could not remember how to use the device. It was at that moment that it rang in my hand. A lady from the congregation was calling. I told her I needed help. She called for an ambulance.

I was taken to the hospital and screened for

My Prayer Journey: Lessons Learned

brain bleeds and stroke. In the end, they found nothing definitive. However, I was left feeling extremely fatigued and with numbness on the left side of my face for the next eighteen months. I tried to return to work a week later, but it was impossible. It was during that week that God sent an angel in the form of one of my patients.

Kelly was a warm and friendly man I had known through the clinic for some time. As I was bringing him back to an exam room, he asked me how I was. My perfunctory reply came, "I'm fine." He said, "I don't think you are." Kelly told me he was stepping out of his box but insisted that I tell him what was going on. Immediately, I broke down and started to weep. The words spilled out as I rehearsed to him the responsibilities that I was carrying and that I didn't feel I could go on but not having a clue what to do about it. Here I was, the nurse, and the patient was reaching out to help me. He told me I needed to take a break and maybe get some counseling. I explained I could not afford to quit my job or to pay for anything not covered by my insurance.

The next day when I arrived at work, I found an envelope in my mail slot filled with twelve, one-hundred-dollar bills, a letter that included directions to a Lake Huron home that was offered to us free of charge for a week, and the number to a counselor, that was also paid for.

As the story goes, we kept that week's

appointment. The home was a beautiful lakeside estate, all the details taken care of, including freshly baked cookies in the cookie jar. Every morning Mark and I met with a Christian counselor who helped us to learn to 'be' rather than 'do.' He guided us through some internalized weights of responsibility and helped me to see how to let go of things I was not required to be carrying. That week changed me. It saved me.

I never went back to work full-time. We went without insurance for a while and then joined a health sharing ministry. I did continue with the district appointment for the next eight years, and it was an experience that was directed by God.

Lesson Learned: God feels our desperation.

> Fear thou not; for I am with thee: be not dismayed; for I am thy God: I will strengthen thee; yea, I will help thee; yea, I will uphold thee with the right had of my righteousness.
>
> Isaiah 41:10 KJV

My Prayer Journey: Lessons Learned

41

The ringing of the phone had been seemingly incessant. My repetitive trips to the lobby to bring my next patient back to the pain suite were tiring. As I sat down to catch up on my computerized charting and carrying out doctor's orders for the day, I took a deep breath. Glancing at my watch, I still had two hours until the office closed. It was going to be a long afternoon.

My long-time supervising doctor sat behind me tapping out his narratives and responses to patient requests and phone calls. My relationship with Dr. Beatty was forged over more than twenty years of working side by side. We had talked many times about our families, our careers, and current events. It was always my delight to share with him regarding my church and Pentecostal ways. Monday morning greetings often included, "What happened at church yesterday?" During these talks, he shared with me about his childhood in southern California when he was a young boy. He had a neighbor who attended a Pentecostal church there, and he had visited with his friend several times. He once told me, "I was always sort of afraid of those services I attended, watching the people worship, run, and shout." I totally understood, and we were able to laugh together. There were times, during the early years, when Dr. Beatty attended some of our services, and that was always thrilling.

Through time and circumstances, the opportunity for such discussions waned. I missed those dialogues about God and church. Strangely though, that afternoon became quiet. The phone sat silent and uncommon no-shows piled up. As I turned in my desk chair toward him, I felt the Lord's presence. We suddenly had some time on our hands, and there was a peculiar stillness, as even co-workers seemed to vanish from the area.

I began to share an example of our need for the Lord that had never come to my mind before. I talked about our soul being the breath of God. I explained that when God created Adam, the Bible says that God breathed into him, and he became a living soul; that our soul is God-shaped, and only more of God can fill that void created by God's breath. If we can picture the ball-shaped toy that children learn to put matching shapes into, we know that the shapes have to be specific to the hole. Many times, people try to press other shaped things into their souls to find satisfaction. No matter how hard we try, we cannot hammer a triangle into a round space. It is like that with our souls. Alcohol won't fit. Immorality doesn't match. Drugs, money, or fame cannot fit into the space of

My Prayer Journey: Lessons Learned

our soul. Only Jesus can fill the longings of our soul.

As I finished my "lesson" and observed Dr. Beatty swallowing back a lump in his throat, and blinking his tear-filled eyes, I was so grateful that I was able to share my faith with him once again. Now that I am retired, that is a special moment I will always cherish. The clinic chaos resumed. It was almost as if God had sealed off a few moments, without interruption, for us to dialogue about my Savior once again.

That is how so many of us found Christ: at the right moment, someone shared with us Christ's love. We must trust that the seeds of the gospel we share with others will somehow be watered and will germinate, grow, and produce fruit in the lives of those whom we encounter.

Lesson Learned: God can interrupt our day to plant or water His seeds.

> I planted the seed in your hearts, and Apollos watered it, but it was God who made it grow.
> I Corinthians 3:6 NIV

Notes

My Prayer Journey: Lessons Learned

42

I heard Him speaking clearly, I would never see my dad again! It was chilly for a late September morning. I hurried into the church in the twilight and started my laps of praise around the auditorium of our church. I was accustomed to this motion of circular prayer, as I had started the practice many months earlier. I would arrive early, just before dawn, make my way into the dark sanctuary, flip on the altar lights, walk, and pray. As I inquired of the Lord about my day's agenda and acknowledged Him so that He would order my steps, I would feel Him move in close and we would walk in tandem. He would lead, and I would follow, around and around, praying for whatever and whomever came to mind.

That particular morning was different from all the rest and is forever etched into my memory. As I came around the northwest corner of the pews, the Lord stopped and said something that was off the subject. He said plainly and clearly in His still small voice, "You will never see your dad again. But remember, precious in My sight is the death of My saints."

That statement stopped me dead in my tracks! What?!? I will never see my dad again? I immediately ceased the circuits and sat on the nearest pew. I grabbed my Day-Timer and began to flip pages to see when I could go to my parents' home. We were scheduled to make a visit in November, but I had to go sooner. I panicked. The schedule for home, the church, and the district were booked solid. What was I going to do?

With this announcement, I gathered my things and headed out the door. I didn't want to be late for work. I had a busy clinic schedule, and from the time I entered the employee entrance until I clocked out at night, the days were always full and demanding. Even so, the Lord's revelation hung around the recesses of my mind and at times, as we often do, I tried to discount it. Surely this was not God's voice. I wrestled with the content of His message wishing it to be wrong but knowing in my heart of hearts what He had said without a stutter.

On the way home that evening, I again tried to figure out some days I could travel to Illinois. I had not comprehended His first statement, "You will never see your dad again."

I came home tired as usual, made dinner, tried to call my dad, but mom said he was in the garden. She reported he had enjoyed a very good day, eaten a good supper, and was now, as I have already stated, in his beloved garden. I said I would try to call him back the next day.

My Prayer Journey: Lessons Learned

Weary, I made my way to bed. Unusual for me, I quickly fell into a deep sleep. Three hours later, around 12:30, I was suddenly awakened by the loud ringing of our home phone. Before my feet hit the floor, I knew what the caller would say to me.

Janet, my younger sister, was calling to inform us that dad had suffered a severe stroke. He died before the sun came up that morning.

I was blessed to have had a warning from my Friend. I was also comforted to know that He was treasuring my dad, and that he was precious in His sight.

Lesson learned: When God speaks, He does not stutter.

> As for God, his way is perfect: the word of the LORD is tried: he is a buckler to all those that trust in him.
> Psalm 18:30 KJV

Notes

My Prayer Journey: Lessons Learned

43

I always adored my dad. I never remember ever fearing abuse or abandonment. He was a strict father, wanting order and expecting obedience. The few times that this compliant-child ever crossed him and received the quick sentencing of discipline, broke my heart. I never wanted to disappoint him.

I have memories of shopping trips, family reunions, and vacations that are memorialized in Kodak Instamatic pictures. He provided for us and protected us in a possessive way that now, looking back on it, was not overkill but genuine concern and love for his four "jay-birds:" Jo, Jean, Jane, and Janet.

When I reached the age of sixteen—his guideline for dating permission—he was still very particular about who that date was with, where it would take us, and what time we would be home. Our curfew was 10 pm, a whole hour or two before most of our friends. At the time, we felt like he thought we were babies, but now we know the wisdom and protection of that decision.

My dad had come so far spiritually during

my lifetime. After his retirement at 56, he began a transformation that was thrilling to watch. He began reading his Bible daily, attended church whenever the doors were open, gave generously in the offerings, and worshipped more openly. I had a front row seat to the "…old man passing away and all things becoming new…" (II Corinthians 5:17).

As an adult, my childhood adoration became admiration for the man I called my dad. His eulogy was filled with high praise for his honesty in business, his integrity, and his love for God and his family. Many people filed past his coffin to report how much this gentle and quiet man was esteemed and honored.

I miss him even now, all these years later, but I learned in the process that as God took away my earthly father, He would prove to be my Heavenly Father.

After dad left, the void that I felt was eased by calling out to the Lord—"My Father!" The Comforter truly carried me through that time of grief.

My Prayer Journey: Lessons Learned

Lesson Learned: He would not leave me alone in my grief.

I will not leave you comfortless: I will come to you.
John 14:18 KJV

When my father and mother forsake me, the Lord will take me up.
Psalm 27:10 KJV

Notes

My Prayer Journey: Lessons Learned

44 I am sitting alone in a hotel room. The plan is to get caught up on some much-needed rest. I have slept nine and a half hours and can't remember the last time that has happened. Even so, I am still a bit lethargic, and I procrastinate getting dressed. I pick up my computer to write another essay for this book, and I hear His voice whisper, "Jane, spend a little time with Me first." I lay aside the computer and sit still and quiet, whispering words of love to my Father, my Creator, my Savior. I pick up my Bible and read a few chapters in my BREAD (Bible Reading Enriches Any Day—read the Bible through in a year) designation for the day. I read some chapters in Numbers, check some commentaries, give some thought to what I have read, then once again, "Let's talk."

I lay aside my Bible, close my eyes, and again begin to enjoy prayer intimacy. I feel His arms wrapping around my tired body and the warmth of His embrace in my spirit. I am realizing His desire for relationship with me, divine relationship. Relationship that only comes from spending quality and quantity time together.

He begins to remind me of His desire for companionship that will culminate when He, the Bridegroom, comes for His bride, the church. He whispers His great love that has been born through the ages. As I sit in His warm embrace, these words are penned as He dictates this poem to me.

Waiting For Love

Long before time began,
In the darkness of the eons,
I longed
For my adoring love to be returned.

In My awesomeness and power,
I caught My life-giving breath,
When the bride of eternity
Came into view of My plan.

She would cost Me My throne-room.
Subjection to flesh and blood,
Submission to My own creation,
On a cross, heart-breaking pain.

Although the cost would be extreme,
So would the love that would be exchanged.
The plan was put in motion, in Bethlehem,
And I never looked back.

My Prayer Journey: Lessons Learned

Six thousand years of waiting
For My bride's preparation.
The garment's fitting is almost complete.
Soon My wait will be ended.

Lesson Learned: He wants a personal, divine relationship with me.

The Lord is my strength and my shield; in him my heart trusts, and I am helped; my heart exults, and with my song I give thanks to him.
Psalm 28:7 ESV

Notes

My Prayer Journey: Lessons Learned

45

I have a sweet memory of the day that Jesus smiled directly at me.

Mom was born, the last of five children, during the depression. She was eight years younger than her closest sibling. Her mother was forty-five years young when my mom made her entrance into this world. Grandma had been introduced to the Pentecostal way by her newly baptized-in-Jesus-Name father-in-law when my mom was eight years old. The next year mom was baptized of the water and the Spirit in a revival meeting.

My mom was the best: the best cook, the best mom, the best example. She was a loving and caring mother and grandmother. She was healthy, strong, and hard working. Mom spent many hours in her "prayer chair" reading the Word and praying for her children and their children. She interceded for the lost and prayed for her church family and beloved pastors.

Her scary diagnosis of pulmonary fibrosis promised an agonizingly slow, suffocating death. Why Lord? After her diagnosis, I soon committed to going to be with her regularly each month to assist my sisters, Jean (who had selflessly come from Tokyo) and Janet, in her care. Janet, being a hospital nurse for many years, was not only capable but loving and kind. Working full time and coming home to increasingly heavy care-giving needs took its toll on her. She never complained. She proved her steadfast Holy Ghost experience many times over during those trying months.

    One particular Thursday morning, I quietly backed my hybrid out of the garage into a sub-zero darkness, illuminated by a waning crescent moon in a cloudless sky. As I glanced at it over my shoulder, I thought it looked like a crooked smile. As was my practice, I thanked God for it. His creation is beautiful and is a gift that I take note of on purpose. Thank You for the beautiful sparkling stars, the light of the moon, the warmth of the sun. Thank You for the crunch of the snow under my feet, the smell of spring rain, the deepest green of springtime grass, and the bright yellow of the daffodils. Whatever creation I look upon, I give thanks. That day, I smiled back and gave thanks for that smile in the dark sky.

    I was facing a seven-hour trip alone in the car as I had done multiple times before. My mom's condition was worsening. I dreaded going and then could hardly drag myself away when it was time to go back home. It would be a long trip. I was tired. I was dreading the day. I connected my phone, hit the music icon, and placed it on shuffle.

My Prayer Journey: Lessons Learned

The lyrics of the first song that played that morning was placed on repeat for the next seven hours.

> Lord I saw Your face last night, when I looked in the sky, You were SMILING!
> You told me it would be ok.
> You would make a way,
> In my dark times.
> Every time I hear Your voice, every time I feel Your touch,
> Lets me know that I can face tomorrow, one more time.
>
> Song, One More Time, on the album One More Time, by the Katinas

I had heard the song before but had not listened to it for a long time. How special I felt that dark, cold morning when Jesus smiled directly at me and serenaded me with a song to match.

We are never alone. He will show Himself to us in His creation. He will embrace us on dark mornings when the day and its agenda loom ahead.

Lesson Learned: I am never alone.

Fear not, for I am with you; be not dismayed, for I am your God; I will strengthen you,

I will help you, I will uphold you with my righteous right hand.
Isaiah 41:10 ESV

My Prayer Journey: Lessons Learned

46

This day is different. I am physically and emotionally exhausted after almost a week of caring for my invalid mother. She is dying a slow and agonizing death from the suffocation of COPD. My nearly 86-year-old, precious mother was never sick a day in her life. She took few prescription medications, had no serious diagnoses, and yet here she is slowly being extinguished. Already, only a shell of her former self, tells me through eyes sunken into the sockets, "I am a prisoner in my own body." My heart cracks at this declaration. I want my precious mom to be set free. What can I do?

Sitting with her, reading the Word or devotionals, and holding her hand does not bring the comfort I so long to provide. Executing all the comfort measures my nurse brain can conjure makes no difference. As time slows in those horrible hours and days, mom wants us to be quiet, saying, "Talking sucks the air out of the room." Her misery suffocates me. My heart seems to be cracking into a million pieces as her lungs become stone.

I struggle. How can this be happening to my prayer-warrior mom? Why is she suffering so? Why? Why? Why?

I ask the Lord to heal her. I beg for her lungs to be filled with **His** breath of life. I plead for Him to take her, and yet she still sits in various chairs, propped up with gel cushions and rolled towels, covered with four blankets and heating pads to stay warm. God, please help her! My mom asks for prayer for breath, for oxygen, "Jane, I can't breathe."

I pray some more, with groanings. No words come.

Then a still small voice. "Suffering has eternal value, trust Me. You cannot see it from your perspective."

Really, Lord? Suffering has eternal value? I muse His words. His suffering certainly has eternal value for the whole world. But how can my mother's suffering have eternal value. The old song comes to mind, "We will understand it better by and by."

So today is different. Although I cannot and may not understand the value of suffering in this life, and I cannot jump up and down waving my hands to be chosen for it, I can pray today, "Thy will be done on earth, in my mother, in me, and in my sisters as we walk through this valley of the shadow of death. Your will be done, Lord."

Fellow traveler, if your road is too rough and

My Prayer Journey: Lessons Learned

your way miserable, I encourage you to find a place to trust Him with your unanswered 'whys.'

Lesson Learned: His ways are above my ways.

> For my thoughts are not your thoughts, neither are your ways my ways," declares the Lord. "As the heavens are higher than the earth, so are my ways higher than your ways and my thoughts than your thoughts.
> Isaiah 55:8-9 NIV

Notes

My Prayer Journey: Lessons Learned

47

Sitting on our couch, wrapped in a thick, fleece blanket that once belonged to my boys (it has multi-colored dinosaurs on it), I was slowly shedding the grogginess of sleep with my second cup of coffee. The morning was Covid-19 quiet, and I was entering my third day of fasting. I knew the virus had not been caused by God, because death is the wages of sin. But here we were right in the middle of this pandemic, and as He always does, He was using our circumstances to bring about some good in our lives.

What good could come from the quarantine of this pandemic? All of the distractions had been removed. After years of merry-go-round living, everything had come to a screeching halt. What would I do with this time? I would pray and fast to draw closer to my God and Savior!

As my husband and I read from the Word of God and then began to pray, we were both easily set free in our spirits to march right in to our prayer zones. Fasting food brings your body under subjection and allows you to feel and hear the Spirit with less hindrances. It gives you a spiritual acuity and opens your ears to be more keenly sensitive.

That morning, as my praise began to flow and I was able to cry out at the brazen altar of repentance, I was propelled into a time of intercession for man: backslidden loved ones, co-workers, and many family members were interceded for that morning.

After nearly an hour, as I began to sit quietly before the Lord to listen for His voice and instruction, He reminded me of an example I had once used in leading our ladies' prayer group more than twenty years prior. Miracle of miracles, I was able to locate it on my computer. He impressed me to post it on my Facebook page. That post was replied to and reacted to more in 24 hours than anything I had ever posted. Here it is:

Thoughts during my morning devotions...

"Getting Ready Today, Moving Out Tomorrow."

Over the past couple of years, when I was making monthly trips to my mother's, I started packing less and less; from several outfits, shoes, and just-in-case-things, to just the essentials—the very least that I would need. It simplified the whole process. What were the essentials?

In an essay entitled Expedition to

My Prayer Journey: Lessons Learned

the North Pole, the author described the provisions carried by the early 19th century explorers. (An Expedition to the North Pole, The Reverend Morgan Allen, June 14, 2020)

Each sailing vessel carried an auxiliary steam engine and a twelve-day supply of coal for the entire projected two-or-three years' voyage. Instead of additional coal, the ships made room for a 1,200-volume library, a hand organ playing fifty tunes, China place settings, cut glass goblets, and sterling silver flatware. The expedition carried no special clothing for the arctic, only the uniforms of Her Majesty's Navy.

Years later, Eskimos came across frozen remains of the expedition, men dressed in their finery and pulling a lifeboat laden with place settings and chocolate.

Their naïveté is beyond comprehension.

How like them are we? We are travelers to a place we have never been before and have no one to ask who has been there. Are we packing carelessly, dragging useless baggage and leaving out things that will insure our safe arrival?

God's Word is clear. All that is here—when it is all over—is wood, hay, and stubble and is reserved unto fire. But what we invest in our soul is as gold.

What are you packing for your journey to

heaven? The Bible gives us a list of essentials:

Repentance, Baptism in Jesus' Name, being filled with the Holy Spirit, walking righteously, prayer, Bible study, being separated from the world in our actions, speech, and dress. These are inexpensive things to pack; Jesus paid for all of it!

What is in your suitcase?

Lesson learned: All things work together for good.

And we know [with great confidence] that God [who is deeply concerned about us] causes all things to work together [as a plan] for good for those who love God, to those who are called according to his plan and purpose.

Romans 8:28 AMP

My Prayer Journey: Lessons Learned

48

Once again, I found myself kneeling at the front pew of our church in the pre-dawn hours. It was familiar. I entered into the Presence of the Most-High God easily on that cool October morning. As I talked with Him about my cares, my longings, and gave thanks in faith that all of it will be cared for, I was directed in the Spirit in repentance. I searched my heart and repented for a bad attitude over a disagreement with my husband the day before. I purposed in my heart to live that day better, more accommodating, and asked myself as I have many times in the past, "What can I do to make his day better?" I continued to search my heart and asked the Lord if there was anything there that needed dealing with. He showed me a replay of a day long ago in the decade of my twenties. It was vivid, detailed, and the memory was seen in living color. I had not remembered the event for years, but in that moment, I understood it was unrepented.

As I verbalized my sorrow over the event, the Lord graciously forgave as He always does. I finished my prayers and headed out for the day. I really don't recall too much about the rest of the day or the schedule that I kept, but as the evening was closing in, I was fatigued and ready to "call it a day." I turned back the coverlet and fluffed my pillows, and I began as usual verbalizing my thanks for the blessings of the day. I thought back over the day and remembered my morning prayers. As I thanked Him for the peace that accompanies true repentance, I tried to recall the long-ago event that He had brought to my mind that morning. I could not remember at all one detail other than I was in my twenties and it was vivid. I searched through the memories and could not recollect anything about it. Nothing. Zilch. Then that still small voice. "That's how it is for me, I cannot ever remember anything about your sins."

Lesson Learned: What can wash away my sin? Nothing but the blood of Jesus!

> How much more shall the blood of Christ, who through the eternal spirit offered himself without spot to God, purge your conscience from dead works to serve the living God?
> Hebrews 9:14 KJV

My Prayer Journey: Lessons Learned
Conclusion

This book has been a dream. It was birthed in my heart over a period of years. In my story-telling discussions with my sisters, often JoElla would reply, "Jane, you need to write a book." Usually this was in response to a funny event from the day I had shared that had made her laugh. Working as an RN in pain management for most of my career, there have been multiple occurrences that have elicited, "we need to write a book." However, the funniest things in life are hard to retell a lot of times, you have to be there to really find the humor, and the stories from my professional life are restricted under HIPPA. As my life has unfolded, I have found my passion in prayer and have decided those experiences are the ones that needed to be committed to the written word. But one trip to the Christian aisles in book stores reveals a multitude of books on the subject. What is left to be said?

One day in the backstage prayer room at Calvary Tabernacle I was getting ready to go out to lead that year's annual ladies conference. As we lined up according to cue, Holly, a friend from the committee, came into my personal space and looked deeply into my eyes and succinctly stated, "Write a book!" then retreated to her place in line. Something struck my heart, and I silently answered, "Yes I will." That's been about five years ago.

I started writing on secluded days spent in our cabin on the church camp ground. But a large percentage of this book has been written sitting at my one-hour vacation spot, Main Street Roasters, Nappanee, Indiana. I have enjoyed gallons of their wonderful flavored coffees, partaken of their lunch specials, and most of all received warm smiling welcomes and inspiration as I have recalled my prayer journey now committed to this book.

If you have read these essays to this point, I thank you for your audience and endurance. It is my hope that, as I shared my heart, you learned some lessons about our God and how He has related to me over the pages of my story. If you read and saw your name or recognized your appearance in my journey, I surely hope my memories or perceptions were not offensive to you. If you are a friend or acquaintance that has known me but never really understood me or how I chose to live my life, please read just a few more paragraphs.

I believe that the Bible is the divinely inspired Word of God. I believe that, in the end of the age, the lives we lived in this brief sojourn called life will be judged according to His Word.

My basis for salvation is found in the book of Acts. Read the whole book and follow the instructions given. You will experience the very best of God by obeying Acts 2:38 and living your

My Prayer Journey: Lessons Learned

life to please the Lover of your soul, the Creator of the universe. Please understand that the epistles Paul wrote in the New Testament were to people who already had the Acts experience of repentance, being baptized in Jesus Name, and the infilling of the Holy Ghost with the evidence of speaking in other tongues as the Spirit gave them the utterance.

The reasons for the way I dress, my uncut hair, and not adorning myself with jewelry or make-up are also scripturally based. See Deuteronomy 22:5; I Corinthians 11; I Peter 3:3; Jude 1:8.

It is my hope that you, too will share my story and the lessons I learned on the road to my relationship with our Heavenly Father. His stories are the best!

Special Thanks

Thanks to all who have inspired and supported me in this endeavor. Namely, my beloved husband, Mark, my three treasured sisters, JoElla, Jean, and Janet. And my editors: my son, Nathan, and my friends, Cammy Kondas, Holly Stewart, and Nancy and Larry Arrowood.

Printed in the USA
CPSIA information can be obtained
at www.ICGtesting.com
LVHW021914051223
765750LV00011B/358